S0-BYS-712

Scribe Publications
JOURNALISM ETHICS FOR THE DIGITAL AGE

Denis Muller was a journalist for 27 years, 22 of them at *The Sydney Morning Herald* and *The Age*, where he held senior editorial positions, including chief sub-editor and news editor at the *Herald*, and associate editor at *The Age*. As assistant editor (investigations), he also established the investigative reporting unit at the *Herald*. Since leaving newspapers in 1993, he has managed an independent research consultancy, and taught in the political science program at Melbourne University. He now teaches media ethics and law in the university's Centre for Advancing Journalism. His doctoral thesis was entitled 'Media Accountability in a Liberal Democracy'. He is also the author of *Media Ethics and Disasters: lessons from the Black Saturday bushfires*.

For Catherine, Jacqueline, Elizabeth,
and Brendan

JOURNALISM ETHICS

for the Digital Age

Denis Muller

SCRIBE

Melbourne • London

DiPietro Library
Franklin Pierce University
Rindge, NH 03461

Scribe Publications Pty Ltd
18–20 Edward St, Brunswick, Victoria 3056, Australia
50A Kingsway Place, Sans Walk, London, EC1R 0LU, United Kingdom

First published by Scribe 2014

Copyright © Denis Muller 2014

All rights reserved. Without limiting the rights under copyright reserved
above, no part of this publication may be reproduced, stored in or introduced
into a retrieval system, or transmitted, in any form or by any means (electronic,
mechanical, photocopying, recording or otherwise) without the prior written
permission of the publishers of this book.

Typeset in Adobe Caslon 11.5/15pt by the publishers
Printed and bound in Australia by Griffin Press

 The paper this book is printed on is certified against the Forest
Stewardship Council® Standards. Griffin Press holds FSC chain of
custody certification SGS-COC-005088. FSC promotes environmentally
responsible, socially beneficial and economically viable management of
the world's forests.

National Library of Australia
Cataloguing-in-Publication data

Muller, Denis, author.

Journalism Ethics for the Digital Age / Denis Muller.

9781922070951 (paperback)
9781925113167 (e-book)

1. Journalists–Professional ethics. 2. Journalistic ethics.
3. Journalism–Objectivity. 4. Online journalism–Moral and ethical aspects.
5. Digital media–Moral and ethical aspects.

070.57973

PN
4756
.M84
2014

scribepublications.com.au
scribepublications.co.uk

CONTENTS

PREFACE

IN 1984, HAVING been a journalist on *The Sydney Morning Herald* for 15 years, I found myself news editor. Five floors up in the newspaper's grimy, greenish-grey citadel in Broadway, I was remote from personal contact with the world. All I knew about what was happening in it I got second-hand through the news copy that was the currency of my professional life. It was a demanding, rewarding, but ultimately bloodless existence. I did not deal personally with the people caught up in the dramas, triumphs, and tragedies that were the subject of this copy — I just made news judgments about them. I dispensed or shared in the making of those judgments, the newspaper came out, and we all moved on to the next day's edition.

Big newspaper offices are like this, especially at the senior editorial level — autocratic, impersonal, detached, focused. They deal with news that is at once real and abstract: real in the sense that an event actually happened, but abstract in the sense that it happened to someone else, somewhere else. The editorial executive's job is to assess its relative importance to another abstraction — the people who read the paper, and the general public at large. Then it is a matter of making a series of largely technical and managerial decisions that give effect to those assessments: decisions about deployment of staff, quality of copy, prominence and display of stories, risks presented by legal issues, and stratagems for dealing with the exigencies of production. It is a very internally focused process, and in general it is carried out by people with a high degree of professional commitment under relentless pressure of time.

Back in the 1980s, what drove this commitment? It certainly was not the money. My salary was roughly equivalent to that of someone at the lower end of the state government's senior executive service, for a week that seldom comprised less than 70 hours' work. Equally certainly, it was not fame. There were no bylines for editorial executives, and by the time you got there, the novelty of seeing your name in print had long worn off. Nor was it glamour. There was no glamour in a day spent inside a vast fluorescent-lit newsroom, dinner in a staff dining room or canteen, and — in the days of letterpress printing — the late evening spent in a cavernous composing room that was noisy, hot, smelly, and dangerous.

No, the commitment came from three psychological drivers. One was the thrill of being caught up in the miraculous urgency of daily newspaper production, culminating in the late-night thunder of the press room, where vast press lines, two storeys high and 50 metres long, turned flying streams of newsprint into thousands of folded newspapers every hour. Another was the sense of self-importance that came from being part of something powerful. The third was the sense of vocation that came from having a defined and recognised function in society — that of the journalist discharging a public duty, fulfilling what was thought of as the 'fourth estate' function of the press: being a watchdog on those in power, and holding them to account.

While I was conscious of being part of something powerful and important, it never occurred to me that I personally wielded power beyond my own internally focused executive power. I certainly had no sense of wielding a public power.

Consequently, I had no sense that I should be publicly accountable. My responsibilities and accountabilities were to the editor. I just got the paper out — or at least did my bit in that direction — as I had for years.

So it was a searing experience to discover, in this relatively exalted position of news editor, that there were people out there who considered that I was, in fact, publicly accountable — or at least the *Herald* was — and that for these purposes I was now the embodiment of the *Herald*. And the issues I was confronting were not the legal ones I had been used to dealing with in my previous position as chief sub-editor, but ethical ones. No one had prepared me for this. In those far-off days when I had been a reporter, I had always tried to treat people decently and to write accurately, but this was my own personal way of doing things. Now I was representing the newspaper itself. What were the newspaper's ethics? What were its views about being accountable to the public? These matters were not part of the internal conversation.

Not that my colleagues were unethical. Quite the reverse. So far as I could tell, they were men and women of great personal integrity and high professional standards. But ethical questions were seldom raised head-on, and were never discussed in detail. They were touched on elliptically, embedded in questions such as: 'Do you reckon this stands up?' Or, 'Have we spoken to this bloke?' Those were questions about verification and fairness, but that was not how they were framed, and the way they were framed did not admit of any general discussion about standards of proof or fairness of portrayal. They were questions directed specifically at the copy in hand, with the object of making a decision about it and then moving on.

As for public accountability, it was simply not part of the conceptual framework within which we worked. If anything, it was regarded as a quasi-political issue that the proprietors could engage with if they wished. On one occasion, a proprietor did so. He was Ranald Macdonald, managing director of *The Age*, and he said on television that he thought newspapers should be accountable to the public. One of my senior colleagues was appalled by this, referring to Ranald as 'that hair-shirt-wearing bastard'. For that colleague, at least, agreeing to be publicly accountable was the equivalent of mediaeval monastic self-punishment, but he did not say why, and no one asked.

So, coming from within this environment, I was ill-prepared for a complaint from a distinguished Australian author whose name I can recall but whose complaint I cannot. We had a telephone conversation in which he was masterful in argument, and I could not string two words together. It was obvious that his complaint had substance, so I took a note and went off to discuss it with the staff member involved. It was not someone I knew well, being from what we ruffians of the news department referred to derisively as Poets' Corner, whose inhabitants wrote book reviews and long features for the Saturday paper. This person dismissed the complaint with a wave of the hand as a difference of interpretation, and who was I to argue? I rang the author back to convey this response. He was even silkier in his deployment of the English language than he had been before, and rang off. Though I never heard another word about it, the experience embarrasses me still — not just for my personal inadequacies, but for what it showed me about the attitude within my profession to the idea of accountability. In this great fortress of a building, behind this authoritative masthead of Gothic script, shielded by switchboards and secretaries and factotums of every description, we felt untouchable.

Well, those days are gone forever. No building or masthead or layers of bureaucracy can shield anyone from the accountability exerted by the digital revolution, which is simultaneously knocking down the walls, devaluing the mastheads, and thinning out the personnel. Nor should it, anyway. The old system worked as it did because of an asymmetry of power: the individual against the newspaper company. Even a distinguished author, who might be thought to have a little more power than the ordinary citizen, could not get justice, even from a newspaper that claimed a sacred trust with its readers.

In later years, my lesson from the experience with the author would be reinforced when I was required to appear as the editorial advocate of the *Herald* — and later of *The Age* — at hearings of the complaints committee of the Australian Press Council. In other words, I was there to answer for the newspaper. There was a pattern to these matters. Some person or organisation would be aggrieved by an article, and would ask the paper for redress. They would be rebuffed, often peremptorily, just as my author had been. They would then lodge a complaint with the Press Council. Much futile correspondence would ensue, and finally the matter would be referred to the complaints committee for adjudication. Then I would get the file. It would show an original complaint — usually having some merit — on a matter of great importance to the individual, but of little wider public importance. The newspaper would have invested some time and ingenuity in attempting to discourage or appease the complainant, short of actually offering to acknowledge and correct the error. By now, it had become for the complainant a matter of principle, and so he or she had gone to the Press Council in search not just of remediation, but of vindication.

This incapacity within newspapers to accept the necessity for public accountability, and to readily correct their mistakes, has become ingrained as part of their culture. The culture is, in turn, the product of several factors. One is the unrelenting focus on the here-and-now of getting the paper out. Another is that in this urgent environment, swift and autocratic decision-making is encouraged. A third is the insulation of editorial decision-makers from the people and events about whom they make their news decisions. A fourth is the institutional protection they have traditionally received by being part of a large bureaucracy. A fifth is that they benefit from being part of something powerful that can generally defeat challenges from all-comers.

And there is something more. To survive in this environment, journalists develop a resilience based on strong self-confidence. To admit fault is to allow a tiny crack to be made in that self-confidence. Newspaper companies understand this, and they understand the consequences for the company and the individual if someone's self-confidence unravels. So in these matters their first loyalty is to the editorial staff, from the editor down. Admirable and indispensable though this is, over time it has blinded the companies and many members of the profession to a competing imperative: in a liberal democracy, those who wield power must submit themselves to public accountability for how they use it.

Neither the media as an industry nor journalists as a professional group have been able to find a way to preserve the psychological impregnability that is essential to sustaining self-confidence while at the same time accepting the requirement for accountability. Their standard response to any proposal for a system for exerting meaningful public accountability has been to rail against it as an attack on free speech. This reveals two things: first, the culture inside the industry continues to see public accountability as anathema; second, as a result of this attitude, industry leaders have not thought hard enough about the matter to have developed anything other than a reflexive and extreme response.

Journalists have an obligation to their personal consciences, and this may require challenges to be made to colleagues, superiors, proprietors, and anyone seeking to bring improper pressure to bear.[1] For everyone involved, however, a foundational problem is that there is little by way of professional ethical consensus to guide them. That leaves individual practitioners and organisations exposed to a kind of relativist jungle in which they are left to make decisions according to their personal or internal ethical compass, without the guidance and support of established professional ethical norms. This itself places a heavy demand on self-confidence, individually and organisationally. The fact that journalists work in such a competitive environment only magnifies the problem.

Nowadays, the digital revolution has confronted a much larger group of people with the same kind of challenges. It has placed the power to publish in the hands of anyone who chooses to do so, while at the same time opening them up to a level of scrutiny that professional media have long been insulated from. An early lesson from the world of online publishing is that this scrutiny can be cruel and uninformed, as well as fair and instructive. It can also be instantaneous.

The digital revolution has another dimension, too. It has created the means by which information can be made globally available from a single source, magnifying exponentially the opportunities to inform the public, but also multiplying the risks of harm. The paradigm case of this is WikiLeaks. This dimension of the digital revolution has added new elements to many established ethical questions that have to be taken into account in contemporary journalism.

The purpose of this book is to help people engaged in contemporary journalism to identify and think through the big ethical questions we face as the digital revolution reshapes the operating environment. I hope that this in turn results in well-reasoned ethical decisions, for the benefit both of those engaged in journalism and the public they serve.

INTRODUCTION

FOR MORE THAN 500 years, from Europe's discovery of printing in about 1450 until the digital revolution at about the turn of the second millennium AD, the power to publish was the preserve of those who had access to a press. From the early twentieth century, this power was extended to those with access to a radio microphone; and from the mid-twentieth century, to those with access to a television studio. These technologies conferred a privilege — the privilege of the platform. This privilege brought responsibilities, which have been laid out in professional codes of journalism ethics. Where radio and television are concerned, they have also been built into government licensing conditions.

The creative destruction wrought on this settled landscape by global digital technology has forced us to confront some fundamental questions. What is journalism? Who is a journalist? What is a media organisation? What will be the new economics of media? What is the relationship between sovereign states and their media? Do the professional norms of journalism have meaning any more? What are the implications for media accountability? What are the opportunities offered by digital technology? What are the risks?

Digital technology now extends the privilege of the platform to anyone with a computer and the skills of basic literacy. This raises large questions of legitimacy and authority deriving from the term 'journalism'. People who work as journalists for established media carry the prestige of those corporations, and this prestige confers legitimacy and authority on their journalistic function. This, in turn, gives them access to people and places — such as the press galleries of parliament, or the press benches of courts — that are not easily accessible, or accessible at all, to other citizens. Whether and how to give institutional recognition to those engaged in journalism outside those corporate structures are questions that are yet to be resolved by our democratic institutions. In the meantime, they have implications for the capacity of non-professional journalists (that is, those who are not attached to an established media outlet) to conduct journalism.

In the world created by the digital revolution, the definition of 'journalist' is more fluid than it once was. For our purposes, this does not matter. As Tom Rosenstiel said, 'Anyone can be a journalist ... The question is whether their work constitutes journalism.'[1] The ethical issues are the same for the self-declared journalist and for the professional. What matters is how we define 'journalism', because of key implicit promises that use of the term conveys to the public. The public will be the victim of deception if merely like-seeming activities are allowed to masquerade as journalism. This is not just about semantics. An early entrant into the ranks of Australia's first bloggers was the writer and commentator Dr Tim Dunlop, who understood the distinction perfectly. Greg Jericho, in chronicling the rise of the Australian blogosphere, recounted this early post by Dunlop in which he described the nature of blogging:

> Let's just say the idea here is to pick apart the issues of the day in the way that normal human beings talk about such things.

This is less about journalism than it is about citizenship, the idea that all of us have a say in how the country is run and that participation is a good thing in its own right.[2]

To engage in journalism, by contrast, is to establish an implicit contractual relationship with the community. This relationship contains promises about factual and contextual reliability, impartiality, and separation of factual information from comment or opinion. If these promises are broken, the community is robbed of something essential to the healthy functioning of democracy: a bedrock of trustworthy information they need so they can make informed choices as voters, consumers, and participants in social life.

And this is only the half of it — think of it as the 'audience' half. The remaining portion is what could be thought of as the 'subject' half — how we treat people in gathering information, how we portray them, how we use the information they give us. If we present ourselves as people who are seeking information for the purposes of journalism, we are making some implicit promises to our subjects, too. These are promises about truth-telling, portraying them fairly, treating them decently, being respectful of them as human beings, and keeping any secrets they confide to us. We are also implicitly promising to use the access we gain to them for the purposes we say we have obtained it — the purposes of journalism — and not for anything else.

Delivering on these promises, both to audiences and subjects, is what gives journalism its legitimacy. Without this legitimacy there would be no reason for society to confer on journalism the privileges it does. But with privileges comes accountability; and already it is apparent, in the way some legal privileges for journalism are being framed, that entitlement to some of those privileges is conditional on the practitioner's signing up to a recognised code of ethics backed by some mechanism of public accountability.

One example can be found in the Commonwealth Privacy Act, which confers certain exemptions on the media; another is in the so-called 'shield' laws that provide some protection for the confidentiality of journalists' sources. The shield laws of the Commonwealth extend this beyond the traditional boundaries of journalism — defined by employment in a recognised media company — to others engaged in disseminating news and information to the public. This is intended to include people who publish on digital platforms. The equivalent laws of the states, however, do not contain this extension: they apply only to employees of media organisations that are signed up to accountability institutions such as the Australian Press Council.

In the digital age, this raises practical as well as theoretical complications.

The practical complication is that if there is no mechanism of accountability to which self-declared journalists can sign up, they will be deprived of privileges that others will receive for doing essentially the same kind of work. More than this, there is no mechanism of accountability for individual journalists in Australia other than being subject to the ethics panel of the Media, Entertainment and Arts Alliance, which is primarily an industrial organisation with limited recognition inside and outside the profession as a body with an accountability function.

The theoretical complication is that this distinction is manifestly unsound, since it is deals differently with people who are doing the same kind of work, when the imperative to be accountable is just as strong for people doing journalism on their own as it is for those doing it as employees of media organisations. Australia has not yet developed institutional arrangements that resolve these complications.

There is another reason for being clear about the meaning of journalism. It is that journalism sometimes entails doing harm — causing pain, hurt, embarrassment, and loss of livelihood or reputation — in pursuit of the public interest, or in placing the public interest ahead of someone's private interest. Ethically, there needs to be a justification for this, which rests on the importance of fulfilling the public-interest functions of journalism.

If our use of the term 'journalism' is to have integrity, then, for all the reasons already outlined, the work done in that name needs to be grounded in the professional ethical framework of journalism. This applies equally to professional journalists and to those who practise journalism in some other capacity. A professional ethical framework provides professional norms. Such norms are essential to good and credible ethical decision-making; otherwise, we have a situation where what is ethical is what any one practitioner thinks is the right thing to do at the time. This kind of relativism helps no one. Professional norms provide a standard, independent of the individual, that can guide an individual's ethical decisions, and against which they can be tested.

However, established professional norms also need to be reconsidered in the light of the digital revolution. Through digital technology, it is possible for huge quantities of information to be made available globally by the keystrokes of a single individual. Obvious examples of this are the leaks of security and diplomatic material by Private Bradley Manning to WikiLeaks in 2010, and by Edward Snowden to *The Guardian* newspaper in 2013. The capacity for global re-publication of material like this to do harm to individuals as well as to national interests, while at the same time providing information to the public on matters of great public interest, confronts us with having to take into account ethical questions of truth-telling, editorial independence, source relationships, censorship, and the harm principle — and to do it on a global scale.

These are matters of applied ethics, and that is what this book is about.

Chapter one examines the WikiLeaks phenomenon, a defining case that crystallises many of the new ethical challenges presented by the digital age. This helps get our bearings: to see what is really new by way of ethical challenges and what are perhaps new angles on old ethical problems. It also helps us make an important distinction — between the *tools* and the *nature* of journalism.

Chapter two describes and discusses the concept of accountability — what the term means in the context of journalism, and the rationale for requiring public accountability by those who practise it. This is related to the question of the nature of the power of journalism.

Chapter three identifies and discusses the values and principles that are reflected in the codes of ethics for journalism. These values are generally common to journalism codes around the Western world, and they have roots in at least four philosophical traditions: virtue theory, social-contract theory, Kantian theory, and utilitarian theory. These theories are described and discussed, and their links with the values of the codes are made apparent.

Chapter four deals with key journalistic concepts that commonly have a bearing on how we make ethical decisions: free speech, censorship, the public interest, and the harm principle.

Chapter five presents a detailed analysis of the concept of impartiality. Discussion of this difficult concept often stops at the statement that bias is in the eye of the beholder, but that is not very helpful. This chapter identifies the elements of impartiality, and demonstrates how it can be assessed.

Chapter six deals with conflict of interest. In the digital age, this is becoming a widespread and difficult problem in journalism, as heritage media look for ways of generating revenue by creating linkages between editorial content and advertising, and new start-ups struggle to find ways of generating income without compromising their expertise or integrity.

Chapter seven demonstrates a useful tool for making ethical decisions. It is based on a modified version of the Potter Box, which was the original creation of a divinity don at Harvard, Ralph Potter, for the purpose of making ethical decisions concerning the atom bomb. Modified slightly for the purposes of journalism, it provides a framework for thinking systematically through ethical dilemmas.

Chapter eight deals with the complex but often neglected question of consent. This is a topic that receives scant attention in the professional codes, but is fundamental to any system of professional ethics, since it is closely bound up with notions of personal autonomy. It is also made more complex in journalism by the fact that there are circumstances where consent is not required.

Chapter nine is about truth-telling, a value that has come under particular pressure in the digital age because of the demands of the so-called 24/7 news cycle, in which the imperative to be first can override the imperative to be right. Parts of truth-telling comprise the narrower but complex issues of verification and standard of proof. These are also discussed.

Chapter ten is about sources and confidentiality. This is without doubt the most high-profile of the ethical issues confronting journalists, and is the one on which there is the highest degree of professional consensus. However, because there are often high stakes involved and the law on the subject is uncertain, the ethical demands it creates can be acute.

Chapter eleven is about deception and betrayal. These are perhaps the most ubiquitous ethical dilemmas in journalism. Indeed, it has been argued that they are so integral to journalism that they are unavoidable. However, there are degrees of deception and betrayal that make a qualitative difference in ethical decision-making, and these are explored in detail.

Chapter twelve is about privacy. This is another high-profile ethical issue, and one on which the profession is frequently vulnerable to criticism. Privacy is multifaceted, having at least seven domains, and these are described and discussed in the context of ethical decision-making. A taxonomy of privacy interests is also presented and discussed.

Chapter thirteen deals with the sensitive fields of disasters and suicides. Reporting on these matters always contains the risk of doing unintended and unjustifiable harm. The risks are discussed, as is good practice for minimising them.

Chapter fourteen is devoted to the way in which ethical issues present themselves in the online environment. While many ethical issues are common to all journalism, online journalism creates new difficulties, as well as some entirely new ethical issues.

Chapter fifteen is about self-care. People engaged in journalism owe an ethical duty to themselves and their families to look after themselves in what can be a physically and emotionally demanding profession. The longstanding culture in which real journalists don't cry still has a strong hold, although change is happening. This chapter deals with those issues, and offers guidance about where to go for help.

Chapter sixteen offers the outline of a code of ethics for the digital age. It draws on existing codes, but takes a broader perspective, and suggests connections between abstract values and decision-making based on the more tangible principles governed by those values. These give us concrete starting points for ethical decision-making.

CHAPTER ONE
LESSONS FROM WIKILEAKS

IN 2006, A new online publisher called WikiLeaks emerged —
in Iceland. The person who was to become synonymous with
it, and is commonly referred to as its founder, was an Australian
citizen, Julian Assange. However, there were other significant
figures associated with its founding, including a distinguished
Icelandic investigative reporter, Kristinn Hrafnsson, who in
2009 revealed the parlous state of Iceland's Kaupthing Bank,
which later collapsed. A former investigative journalist of 20
years' experience who had won Iceland's journalist of the year
award three times, Hrafnsson became the official spokesman
for WikiLeaks.

Thus, from its very beginnings, WikiLeaks was a
journalistic hybrid. Assange had no professional background
in journalism, but Hrafnsson certainly did, and so did Sarah
Harrison, a Briton, who was also among its founding figures.
At first, WikiLeaks disavowed some of the fundamental values
and principles of journalism, including the prior verification
of published material. It also seemed unconcerned by any
potentially harmful consequences of its decisions to publish, or
by the motives of those who leaked material to it. The statement
on its website that declared its criterion for publishing was
broad and bald. WikiLeaks, it said, accepted for publication

'classified, censored or otherwise restricted material of political, diplomatic or ethical significance'.[1]

It thus created what the political scientist and media analyst Professor John Keane has called 'a custom-made mailbox that enabled disgruntled muckrakers within any organisation to deposit and store classified data in a camouflaged cloud of servers'.[2] It is clear from the context that this was not intended as a slur: it appeared in an article based on a long interview with Assange in which the author proffered the observation that Assange could be described as the twenty-first century's Tom Paine, the Anglo-American Enlightenment writer and political activist who championed the triumph of reason and the liberty of the press.

Just the same, Keane's characterisation raised important questions of journalism ethics concerning verification, confidentiality, harm, and motive. These were not the only ethical issues to arise in the WikiLeaks case. For example, what justifies publishing material that has been illegally obtained? And how can editorial independence be preserved in the face of attempts by sources to muscle in on it? WikiLeaks and Assange himself were to come up against these ethical realities in their successive releases of classified military, security, and diplomatic information in 2010.

WikiLeaks started in a spirit of what might be called anti-journalism. It took the view that the established media were complicit with governments and other powerful interests in withholding information from the public that they had the right to know. The journey of WikiLeaks from anti-journalism to sources for journalism illustrates in stark relief the difference in the digital age between an information dump and journalism.

This journey was traced by Andrew Fowler in his biography of Assange,[3] and by Professor Gerard Goggin, chair of the Department of Media and Communications at the University of Sydney, in an analytical narrative published in *Ethical Space*, an international journal of communications ethics, in 2013.[4]

Professor Goggin began by recounting WikiLeaks' publication in April 2010 of secret US military video footage showing an Apache helicopter shooting at and killing about a dozen civilians in Baghdad three years previously. WikiLeaks published the video under the title of *Collateral Murder*. This was clearly a satirical shaft based on 'collateral damage', the US military's euphemism for the killing of civilians. While the footage generated severe criticism of the US military, there was also a backlash against WikiLeaks. It was accused by people in journalism of emotional manipulation and of editing the video in a way that stripped it of important context.

Up until this time, WikiLeaks had made a virtue of what Professor Goggin called its 'fiercely independent' willingness to publish anything that it thought its self-proclaimed mission entitled it to publish. However, its experience in the aftermath of the *Collateral Murder* leak was chastening. It decided to change its tactics in what, for the anti-journalistic WikiLeaks, was a radical turn: it decided that it needed an alliance with journalism.

In July 2010, three months after the release of *Collateral Murder*, WikiLeaks was ready to launch what turned out to be a far more comprehensive and complex release of classified material — US military and security data on the war in Afghanistan. This tranche of material came to be known as the Afghanistan war logs. Rather than go it alone, WikiLeaks this time approached a number of large and respected international newspapers, including *The New York Times*, *The Guardian*, and *Der Spiegel*. Its exact motives for doing so were a matter of speculation, but *The Guardian* published an article by one of its own staff reporters, Dan Kennedy, which might be taken as a good guess:

Of all the questions raised by the Afghanistan war logs, perhaps the most intriguing is this: why would an organisation as independent-minded and disdainful of the traditional media as WikiLeaks seek out those very media as partners rather than going it alone?

My necessarily speculative answer is that WikiLeaks founder Julian Assange, who's made a speciality of revealing embarrassing governmental secrets, learned something important earlier this year. That's when he briefly caused a sensation by releasing a video of a US Apache helicopter firing on Iraqi civilians, killing (among others) a Reuters photographer and his driver.

The lesson: shocking material and a flair for public relations may be enough to get you noticed. But if it's credibility you want, then old-fashioned news organisations still have something to offer.[5]

The credibility that Kennedy was writing about derives from the keeping of those promises to society implied in the term 'journalism'. The scale, sensitivity, and potential harmfulness of the war logs put them in a class of their own for complexity of ethical decision-making, and the editorial staffs of the newspapers brought to bear their experience in established journalistic procedures for dealing with them. These procedures included, in particular, a detailed assessment of the risks involved in publishing — risks to anyone identified in the materials, risks to national security, and risks to the reputations of the newspapers. This approach led to tensions with the WikiLeaks people, who did not seem to appreciate that, in this relationship, they themselves were not the journalists: they were the journalists' sources. It was the newspaper editors who would make the final decisions. This was a resolute assertion of a long-established value in journalism — editorial independence. The newspapers would not be captives of their source, no matter how high-profile he was.

Despite these precautions and the application of established professional journalistic standards, WikiLeaks came under intensive criticism, after the war logs had been published, from organisations such as Reporters Without Borders and Amnesty International for what they said was carelessness in releasing the names of Afghan informants who were assisting the international forces in Afghanistan. There were many subsequent public debates about the adequacy of the pre-publication process undertaken by the newspapers in redacting names and other information tending to identify informants or do other unjustifiable harm. The sheer scale of the war logs made it extremely difficult to be sure that harm had been minimised, and the on-the-ground complexities of the war made it impossible to know with certainty who would be able to draw harmful conclusions from the material. However, the extent of any harm actually done remained a matter of speculation.

In preparing for its third major release of classified material in November 2010 — the US diplomatic cable traffic that came to be known as Cablegate — WikiLeaks again entered into agreements with major newspapers. This time, there were many more newspapers involved, including the Fairfax newspapers in Australia. WikiLeaks had a strategic reason for this. Cablegate contained a lot of material of specific interest to particular countries because it revealed candid, not to say embarrassing, assessments by US diplomatic personnel about those countries and their leaders. So, in addition to enabling it to take advantage of the verification and analytical expertise of the newspapers' journalists, WikiLeaks achieved high visibility in a number of countries, thereby building its profile and potentially attracting new sources of material.

Professor Goggin noted, 'With Cablegate, WikiLeaks found a rapprochement with the press. Indeed WikiLeaks went so far as to cloak itself in the honourable, truth-telling traditions of the fourth estate.'

What do we learn from the WikiLeaks case about the ethics of journalism in the digital age?

First, there is a big difference between an information dump and journalism. Simply availing ourselves of the technology that allows us to publish does not turn our work into journalism. Journalism requires truth-telling. This means verifying that material is genuine, and publishing it in a way that is accurate as to plain facts and context. Failure of contextual accuracy was one aspect for which WikiLeaks had been criticised over *Collateral Murder*.

Second, journalism requires harm-minimisation. It is a breach of the journalistic ethical value of responsibility to publish recklessly, carelessly, and without regard to potential harm. This means taking pains to imagine and assess the possible risks to life, human well-being, property, and reputation, as well as to a particular public interest in having countries able to conduct foreign policy and provide optimum security for their forces engaged in war.

Third, journalism also requires these risks to be assessed against a more general public interest: the interest in knowing as full a story as possible about decisions by governments that commit their societies to grave undertakings, such as war. This includes the public interest in knowing the truth instead of lies. When governments go to war and lie to their people about why, it is a gross betrayal of public trust. There is a corresponding high public interest in revealing the lie, even at some risk of potentially serious harm. These balances are difficult to strike. They are balances that people involved in journalism have a professional ethical obligation to strike conscientiously.

Fourth, journalism also requires that we take into account how the material we rely upon was obtained and, related to that, the motive of the source in supplying it. Material that is reasonably suspected of having been illegally obtained presents obvious ethical difficulties. What justifies publication of such material? In the WikiLeaks case, it was obvious that the material had been obtained illegally because of its classified status. It was equally obvious that it contained matters of great public interest, and that a substantial ethical argument could be made out on public-interest grounds for publishing it. And what was the motive of the leaker? Evidence subsequently came to light that Private Bradley Manning, who supplied the material to WikiLeaks, was motivated by what seemed to be deep disillusionment at the way the US military was conducting the wars in Iraq and Afghanistan, and by a strong desire to see it exposed. WikiLeaks' motives were more clear-cut: publishing this material would fulfil its self-proclaimed mission of bringing governmental secrets to light.

The newspapers, once they had been brought into it, had to make assessments about these motives. It was apparent that the editor of *The Guardian*, Alan Rusbridger, assessed the motives of Assange and of the original source, Bradley Manning, as being grounded in a genuine belief that the public interest would be served by revealing the information contained in the logs about how the war in Afghanistan was being conducted.[6] Yet it was also clear that, even after taking the decision to publish, Rusbridger remained deeply concerned by the ethical dilemmas involved.

One issue that troubled him was that of editorial independence. Rusbridger and his colleagues on the other newspapers learned that it was imperative to assert their editorial independence in the face of pressure from a highly valuable yet capricious and headstrong source who wished to regard himself as an editorial partner rather than an editorial source.

The second issue that concerned Rusbridger was how to assess the risks and benefits involved in publishing this material. He wrote subsequently that while those he called the enemies of WikiLeaks made repeated assertions about the harm done, the reaction from many countries showed a 'thirst for information' of the kind in the logs. Implicit in what he wrote was that, while it was impossible to make an accurate assessment in advance of publication, the evidence afterwards suggested that the benefits outweighed the risks. *The New York Times*, in its efforts to minimise the risk of harm, talked with the State Department, the Pentagon, or the White House before each round of publication. This, too, is ethically challenging. It is a leap of faith to take a government's word on such questions when the material involves an egregious and embarrassing breach of the government's own secrecy. Yet this was done specifically for the purpose of meeting another ethical obligation — that of minimising harm.

In summary, then, there were four big ethical questions for the newspapers handling the WikiLeaks material: whether to deal in material known to have been illegally obtained; how to assess the motive of the original source, Private Manning; how to minimise harm; and how to maintain editorial independence. These are not new ethical questions, but, in the digital age, as the WikiLeaks case showed, they can come with heightened stakes.

The enduring nature of these essential ethical questions was demonstrated by Rusbridger in quoting a memo written 40 years earlier by Max Frankel, the lawyer who supervised *The New York Times* defence in the Pentagon Papers case. The Pentagon Papers revealed secret information about the way the United States was conducting the Vietnam War, and showed that the administration of President Lyndon Johnson had systematically lied to the American people about it. There are obvious parallels in this with the Afghanistan war logs. Frankel's advice can be paraphrased in six points:

1. The media's job is to decide, on the grounds of news values, whether to publish information.
2. If the source has violated his oath of office, it is the job of the authorities to enforce their law or oath without the media's collaboration.
3. All sources are deserving of protection by the media to whom they have entrusted information.
4. It is part of the media's job to reveal the biases and apparent purposes of those who leak.
5. If there is a risk of direct, immediate, and irreparable damage, the media have an obligation to limit what they publish [to minimise the risk].
6. If in doubt, give the appropriate authorities the chance to make their case about the risks.

What is absent from Frankel's advice is any reference to the public interest, although it might be subsumed in the first point. Otherwise, he could be writing contemporary advice for those engaged in journalism.

The WikiLeaks case also helps us reflect on the role of digital-age journalism in liberal democracies. Professor Goggin argues that we need a set of what he calls 'democratic affordances' that enable us to identify how technology can be harnessed to help journalism serve society in the digital age. An 'affordance' is a property of technology that allows it to used for certain purposes. So, in what ways can we use digital technology to enhance journalism in democratic societies?

The WikiLeaks case shows us several ways. One is that

digital technology enables the extremely swift transfer of information, including from sources that can be penetrated more easily by digital means than was possible previously. The contrast between the electronic transfer of the Afghanistan war logs and the laborious photocopying that had to be done by Dr Daniel Ellsberg in leaking the Pentagon Papers to *The New York Times* in 1971 is extraordinary.

So here are two affordances: swift transfer, and readier penetration of secrecy. A third affordance is instant global reach. The Internet provides a worldwide platform of dissemination by which material can be published in text as well as broadcast media around the world simultaneously. A fourth affordance is the provision by social-media platforms of a means by which any person with a mobile device can contribute material on platforms that have a global reach. We have seen this illustrated by the way the street demonstrations of the Arab Spring, exemplified by the 2011 overthrow of Colonel Gaddafi in Libya and of President Mubarak in Egypt, were both fuelled and reported by mobile technology.

Related to this, but applicable more in mature democracies, is a fifth affordance: the use of digital technology to mobilise political participation. An example in Australia was the OurSay organisation, which used online and mobile technology to generate interest in political issues. In the 2013 federal election, the efficacy of this approach was the subject of research by the University of Melbourne's Centre for Advancing Journalism and Centre for Public Policy, to test whether it did in fact make any difference to levels and types of political participation and to the media's reporting of the election campaign. Early indications from the research were that, while digital technology provided an additional platform for people to become engaged in the political process, those who used it tended to be already involved. It also tended to appeal to younger rather than older voters. Overall, it appeared that digital technology did not significantly broaden political participation in a mature democracy, but provided a means of participating that was attractive to younger voters in particular.

A sixth affordance is the provision by digital technology of an instrument of accountability that can be applied not only to those whom the media have traditionally held to account — government and big business — but to the media themselves. Journalists who make mistakes or behave unethically are much more likely to be exposed on blogs and other digital outlets than was the case when they were protected within the citadels of big media companies.

All these affordances potentially have a journalistic dimension because of the centrality of journalism in the dissemination of information, and the exchange of ideas and opinions, without which democracy cannot function. They bring about new ethical challenges — many of which were illustrated by the WikiLeaks case — or new angles on old ethical challenges. They also force us to reconsider the functions of journalism, since it is in the fulfilment of these functions that we find justification for the ethical balances we so often have to strike.

The functions of journalism in the pre-digital era were articulated and developed during the centuries after the invention of earlier technologies — moveable type and the printing press. These functions became clearer in the latter half of the twentieth century, under the influence of the United States Commission on the Freedom of the Press and the growth in journalism scholarship. Kovach and Rosenstiel captured the essentials: 'The primary purpose of journalism is to provide citizens with the information they need to be free and self-governing.'[7]

This may be usefully expanded into about half-a-dozen core functions:

- Providing information that allows the citizen to exercise the choices of citizenship, and to participate in the economy and in the life of the wider community.
- Keeping the citizen up to date with the important things that are happening in the world.
- Helping society to understand itself (the 'mirror' function).
- Providing a forum for the exchange of ideas and opinions (the 'forum' function).
- Being a watchdog on those in power (the 'accountability' function)
- Providing entertainment.

The digital-age affordances described above suggest we can add to this the function of hosting — of providing a means of enhanced democratic participation, by creating a point of direct entry into the public conversation for everyone who wishes to participate. This, of course, brings with it a new dimension on an old ethical obligation — the gatekeeping obligation. Journalism has always required judgments to be made about what to publish and what not to. The torrent of unfiltered material poured into the public domain by the Internet — 'an information wasteland teeming with lies and inaccuracies' — heightens this obligation in the interests of truth-telling and harm minimisation.[8]

In other respects, the affordances suggest a broadening of some of those functions. The 'forum' function can now involve providing a platform for immediate and continuous interactive exchanges by limitless numbers of people in ways that are not constrained by space and time, and that do not require of participants the effort of writing argumentative articles or even letters. A one-sentence response will do. The affordances also increase the scope and immediacy of the accountability function, and add to it a reflexive element that was simply not available before: a means of holding the media to account.

In the digital age, then, we have an additional function for journalism, some enhanced functions, and some new ethical obligations.

CHAPTER TWO
THE CONCEPT OF ACCOUNTABILITY

IN HIS COMMENTARY *On Hallam's Constitutional History*, Thomas Babington Macaulay, the nineteenth-century British parliamentarian, polemicist, poet, and historian, wrote, 'The gallery in which the reporters sit has become a fourth estate of the realm.'

He was referring to the press gallery in the British Houses of Parliament. The estates of the realm — which he was now metaphorically expanding — were the seats of governmental power in nineteenth-century England: the Lords Spiritual, the Lords Temporal, and the Commons. Thus Macaulay was equating the power *informally* acquired by the press with the power *formally* residing in the centre of government. This has since become a synonym for the media, seized upon by the media themselves, and absorbed into the political lexicon of the English-speaking democracies.

The Fourth Estate ideal has long been contested, mainly on the basis that the media is an industry, with critics asking how an industry can credibly fulfil its political functions and its commercial ambitions at the same time.[1] While this is a serious challenge, it does not assert a loss of power on the part of the media — rather, it concerns an apparent perversion of the original motives for exercising that power. The power itself remains.

To understand this power, we need to identify its nature and sources. The nature of media power takes two forms. The central power of the media — sought by anyone who publishes journalism — is the power to portray, to represent people, organisations, ideas, and events to the world. In this way, they construct for their audience a reality and understanding of the world beyond the audience's personal knowledge and experience. A further power is that, even in the second decade of the twenty-first century, when the digital revolution has provided the technological means by which everyone can publish, while at the same time reducing the financial capacity of traditional media to sustain journalism, the media remain a central forum of political communication in modern liberal democracies.

This brings us to the sources of media power. There are two:

- acquired power — which large media organisations have accrued by virtue of their control over the means of information-gathering and dissemination, and
- delegated power — which has been conferred on the media by society in order that they may carry out certain functions central to the workings of a liberal democracy.

Their acquired power has an economic dimension arising from their control of the assets needed to gather and disseminate information and consequently their control of their market. This control affects what is read, seen, and heard by way of editorial and advertising content, and it is this acquired power that is now under threat from the digital revolution.

Their delegated power is given effect through certain privileges: the privilege of the platform; privileges of access to people and institutions; and certain privileges at law, including, in Australia, laws concerning privacy and protection of source confidentiality ('shield' laws). And, in addition to power and privileges, the media have the potential to do excusable harm. All these — power, privilege, and potential for harm — derive from performing the journalistic functions that are recognised and valued by the community. They are thus part of the contract between the profession of journalism and the community, and it follows that anyone who engages in journalism implicitly becomes party to this contract.

Increasingly in democratic societies, those who wield power are expected to account for the way they use it. Political scientists write of 'the public's demand for accountability', of 'an unquenchable thirst for accountability that cuts across the political spectrum'.[2] At the root of this movement is a loss of faith in institutions, giving rise to public suspicions that power is abused and that the public interest is ignored.[3] This applies with particular force to the media. Since the middle of the twentieth century, public-opinion polls have consistently shown low levels of public trust in the media and in journalism.[4]

Even though the term 'accountability' is a slippery one, it seems to have a number of identifiable ingredients. When we talk about holding people accountable, we usually mean making them answerable for their actions or performance, and this usually connotes some form of redress or making amends.

The means for sheeting home these responsibilities generally take the form of laws, regulations, rules, or codes. But they can also take the form of an agreement that focuses on mutual obligations, an implicit compact that is not a legal document but an ethical commitment.[5] A useful way to think about accountability is to consider it as having four dimensions:

1. Who are accountable?
2. Whom are they accountable to?
3. What are they accountable for?
4. How are they accountable?[6]

In 2004, journalists and journalism students in Australia were surveyed on this issue.[7] They were asked: 'To whom do the media owe accountability?' Their answers are summarised in the table below:

Entity or interest to whom accountability is owed	Number of mentions
n = 168	
Unspecified but implies 'the public'	55
The public	44
The reader/audience	18
The craft/industry/codes	12
The people reported about	11
The editor/employer/shareholder	8
The law	3
Regulators	2
Sales	1

Multiple responses were permitted.

It can be seen that by far the broadest consensus among journalism professionals was that the media owe accountability to the public in a general sense, followed by a subset of the public, being the reader or audience.

They were then asked which values, behaviours, and effects the media should be held accountable for. Their answers were:

Value, behaviour, or effect	Number of mentions
n = 168	
Taking responsibility for what is published and for behaving ethically	55
Being fair/balanced/impartial	51
Factual accuracy/completeness	39
Being truthful	32
Transparency of behaviour/explaining actions	21
Correcting errors/making amends	20
Generally discharging a public interest function	13
Being independent of improper or irrelevant influences	13
Protecting sources	3

Multiple responses were permitted.

Clearly, the most widely recognised value was responsibility: being prepared to answer for what is published and for behaviour associated with publication, followed by acting fairly and without conscious bias. Values associated with truth-telling — being factually accurate and conscientious about truthfulness — were also widely recognised as matters for which the media should be held to account.

As matters stand, there are two formal mechanisms of accountability for the media in Australia — the Australian Press Council, and the Australian Communications and Media Authority. Each has limitations concerning (in different ways) scope, powers, transparency of process, sanctions, and public visibility. In 2011–2012, the Australian government conducted two inquiries that addressed this problem.[8] They both recommended some form of statute-based regulation;

but, after an ill-conceived attempt to give effect to these recommendations in early 2013, the Australian government gave up.

However, the digital revolution has started a new means of holding the media to account. This reality is captured in the title of Greg Jericho's book referred to in the Introduction: the rise of the 'Fifth Estate'.[9] Blogging's strengths as a mechanism of accountability are its immediacy and its transparency to a wider audience — albeit only to the audience of particular online exchanges. People engaged in journalism, whether as individuals or as employers of large media organisations, no longer have the hiding places they once had, but their exposure is still limited. The weaknesses of blogging as a mechanism of accountability are that it is not visible to the public beyond the online audience, not based on any form of due process, and not grounded in accountability to a formal and acknowledged framework of ethical obligations. It is, however, a start.

CHAPTER THREE
VALUES, PRINCIPLES, AND ETHICAL THEORIES

IN THIS BOOK, you are going to see quite a lot of the word 'values', because they provide the foundations for ethics. But, because different people mean different things by it, let me start by saying what the word means here.

The common definition itself contains the germ of what I mean when using it. Something we value is something we prize. But our meaning is a metaphysical extension of that. In ethics, we prize something because it is inherently good — it is good in itself and therefore to be upheld, protected, and regarded as morally preferable. One value that we are familiar with, and which is universal, is the sanctity of human life. Another familiar value, more closely applicable to the ethics of journalism, is honesty.

Principles — another word we are going to see quite a lot of — are the general rules that flow from our adherence to a value. So the value of honesty governs the principle that we tell the truth; the value of fairness governs the principle that we portray people in a way that faithfully reflects what we know about them; and the value of respect governs the principle that we do not refer to someone's race or colour or other personal attribute without good reason.

The values that govern the expression of principles in the

codes of ethics for journalism around the Western world are, broadly speaking, these:
- Honesty
- Truth-telling
- Fairness
- Respect
- Independence
- Confidence-keeping
- Transparency
- Responsibility
- Free speech

These are easy to list, but it is not always easy to appreciate fully what each of them means. To make them useful as a guide to good ethical decision-making, I have teased out the principles and practices that flow from them.

Honesty MEANS:
- When we are acting as a journalist, we declare this at the outset.
- We tell our subjects truthfully what the story is about, as best we know it at the time.
- If the story later changes to the person's detriment, we give them a chance to respond.

Truth-telling MEANS:
- We verify information prior to publication.
- We apply a standard of proof proportional to the seriousness of any allegations we report.
- We report facts accurately and in a way that gives a truthful impression of their context.
- We do not exaggerate or 'beat up' the information we have.

- We do not suppress information that people need for a truthful account.
- We give an account that is complete as far as we know it at the time.
- If something later happens that materially alters or adds to what we know, we publish that, too.
- We correct and acknowledge errors.
- Where propaganda content is inextricable from news content, we limit the propaganda content to what is necessary to provide a sufficiently full news account.

Fairness MEANS:
- We portray our subjects in a way that is faithful to the evidence we have about them.
- We avoid inaccurate, malicious, cruel, or bad-faith portrayals.
- We avoid distortion or misrepresentation.
- We do not suppress relevant available facts.
- We offer people an opportunity to reply.
- We separate our comment from our news reporting.
- We obtain prior consent from our subjects, unless the circumstances make it unnecessary.

Respect MEANS:
- We do not make unnecessary references to people's race, colour, ethnicity, religion, disability, gender, sexual orientation, marital status, or other personal attributes.
- We do not intrude on people's privacy.
- We do not intrude on people's grief.
- We do not exploit people's vulnerability.
- We do not exploit people's ignorance of media practice.
- We do not exploit the content of a person's online social networking site without their consent.

Independence MEANS:

- Our decisions about what to publish are based on the journalistic merits of the material.
- Our decisions about what to publish are free of commercial or self-interested considerations.
- Our decisions about what to publish as news have the qualities of impartiality.

Confidence-keeping MEANS:

- We make sure that we, and anyone from whom we obtain information, are agreed about the status of the information as on the record, on background, or off the record.
- Information that is off the record is information received in confidence.
- Information received in confidence may not be published or attributed to its source.
- The identity of the source of confidential information is itself confidential.
- Undertakings of confidentiality, including identity of the source, are binding in all circumstances.

Transparency MEANS:

- We do not deceive people about what we are doing.
- We avoid conflicts of interest; where a conflict exists, we declare it.
- We tell our audience as much about how we got the story as is necessary for them to make an informed evaluation of it.
- We tell our audience if we have paid for information.
- Correction without acknowledgement of error is insufficient.

Responsibility MEANS:

- We are accountable publicly for our journalism.

- We accept the consequences when we make mistakes or errors of judgment.
- In our decision-making, we take into account the risks and benefits to others.
- We do not place our own interests ahead of other people's.
- Any risk of harm to others is proportional to the public interest intended to be served.

Free speech MEANS:
- All people in a democracy have a fundamental right to express their beliefs and opinions
- We also recognise that free speech gives way in some circumstances to other interests, and therefore is not absolute.
- We recognise that journalism is the main means by which free speech is given practical effect in a modern democracy.
- We recognise that the way we do our work as journalists can promote or hinder free speech.
- We promote rather than hinder free speech.

I believe that any departure from these principles and practices is ethically justifiable only in the public interest.

Philosophical foundations

The values and principles that we see in journalism codes of ethics can be traced clearly to at least four of the philosophical traditions that have grown out of, and in turn influenced, Western thought.

Virtue theory

Virtue theory has a long history. It began with Aristotle, who asked the question, What makes someone a good person?

He answered this by saying that a good person was someone who habitually acted in ways that conformed to a great list of virtues. For our purposes, we can list three of these, because they are expressed as values in our codes: honesty, fairness, and respect.

Virtue theory asserts certain universal values that apply to us all, regardless of religion or cultural background, because they arise from our common humanity. This eliminates cultural relativism, on the grounds that there are some things that are always right for all people at all times. It is this breadth and universality that gives virtue theory its strength and relevance.

However, there are limitations to this theory, as there are to all philosophical theories. The main one, for the purposes of journalism, is that on its own it does not help us choose between two right things, which is a choice we often have to make in journalism. Thoughtful application of the values and principles in our codes often involves the striking of a balance, sometimes between benefits and harms, or rights and wrongs, but frequently between two competing things that are right.

For example, it is not uncommon for the values of truth-telling and confidence-keeping to conflict with each other. This particular conflict arises when journalists find themselves bound by a promise of confidentiality, and a requirement — sometimes under threat of imprisonment — to tell the truth in a court of law about the identity of a confidential source. Virtue theory doesn't help us make that choice. We have to look more widely to do so, and by drawing on other lines of philosophical reasoning, we can be helped in thinking our way to a decision.

Social-contract theory

Thomas Hobbes, John Locke, and Jean-Jacques Rousseau — the three philosophers most closely associated with social-contract theory — were concerned with the problem of how human beings could live securely and peacefully in large societies while retaining their individuality and individual rights. The answer to this conundrum seems obvious to us now, living in a constitutional democracy, but it was by no means clear at the time: the English Civil War and the French Revolution had to be gone through before we got here.

Hobbes, an English philosopher and political scientist, lived a long life. He was 91 when he died in 1679, having lived through a turbulent period in English history, including the Civil War. We can only speculate whether the violence of the war influenced his thinking, but what we know for certain is that a major influence on him was the mathematician and astronomer Galileo, whom he met in 1636 during a visit to Florence.

Galileo and the mathematical mode of thinking captivated Hobbes. He was looking for a way to bring certainty into the uncertain domain of moral and political theory, and the certainties and proofs of mathematical method gave him a way to think about how certainty in morals and politics might be created.

Out of this he produced a hypothesis about human behaviour: everything, including human sensation, was caused by motion. Galileo had proposed that motion was the natural state of things — things moved until something stopped them moving. Hobbes applied this idea to the actions of people: they would move and keep moving until something stopped them. Their motion would be dictated by what he called their appetites and aversions — things they desired and things they feared. He also asserted that this would be an unceasing and universal process: all people would restlessly seek to gratify their desires and avoid the things they feared.

Having established his hypothesis of human motion and

the drivers of it, Hobbes then turned to the question of power. He defined a person's power as his or her capacity to obtain some future apparent good. This led him to say that everyone would always seek to have some power, although not every person would seek to acquire the same amount as everyone else. Some people's ambitions might be greater than others'.

Each person's power — he called it 'natural power' — consisted of the amount by which his or her abilities, riches, reputation, and social connections exceeded those of others. And he saw this as a constant push-and-pull between rivals: 'Every man's power resists and hinders the effects of other men's power.'

Today, we call this a zero-sum game: that is, for every gain by one person, there is an equivalent loss by someone else.

So Hobbes saw human society as a contending mass of grasping ambitions, and he wondered how it could be prevented from degenerating into a kind of jungle where the strongest prevailed and where even the strong lived in constant fear of being thwarted or killed.

All these visions and hypotheses he set out mainly in one book, *Leviathan*. Published in 1651, it was the third in a series of books concerning government and society, and it is the one that has carried Hobbes's legacy down to us. It was in *Leviathan* that he introduced his celebrated concepts of the State of Nature, the Right of Nature, the Law of Nature, and the Social Contract.[1]

The state of nature, he said, was what would exist if there were no laws and no means of enforcing them. Based on his hypotheses about mankind's instincts and behaviour, he famously described what he thought such an existence would be like: 'solitary, poor, nasty, brutish, and short'.

The right of nature was the freedom of every person to use whatever power he had to get his own way, and this would lead to the law of nature, in which every person had a right to everything, even someone else's body. This state of affairs he described in another famous formulation as 'a condition of war of every one against every one'.

People, Hobbes said, would eventually seek some better way of living. Reason would lead them to see that each person should give up the unbridled right to do or take anything or violate anybody — provided everyone else agreed at the same time to do the same thing. Thus by a concerted act, all would renounce their rights of nature at the same time.

But this did not solve the problem of how to control people's appetites and aversions. Some force would be necessary to make the agreement stick. And this force, Hobbes proposed, was the people as a whole — 'the whole combined force of all the contractors', as he put it. They would transfer their natural powers to some authority. In doing so, each person would be bound by mutual obligation to respect the supreme civic power of the people as a whole — the Leviathan of the title.

Supreme civic power is what, nowadays, we call sovereignty. Thus, in Hobbes's model, the contract made among all the people — what he called the social contract — exists side-by-side with the idea of the sovereignty of the people. However, Hobbes did not go so far as to assert the sovereignty of the people over that of the Crown; quite the reverse. He remained an absolute monarchist. For him, the supreme civic power would reside in the person of the monarch.

The philosopher who developed the idea of the sovereign people was another Englishman, John Locke. Locke asserted that the centre of power lay in the will of the people, and that government was simply the trustee to which the people delegated authority from time to time (as at elections, for example). Locke's most important work on this topic was first published in 1689, 38 years after Hobbes had published

Leviathan, and one year after the English Revolution had seen William and Mary of Orange installed by the English parliament in place of the last of the Stuarts, James II. This was to usher in an era of constitutional stability in England after the strife-torn years in which the monarchy had been abolished, the Cromwellian commonwealth tried and abandoned, and the monarchy restored.

Even so, it was a dicey time to be writing about sovereignty — especially when it was the sovereignty of the people, and not the sovereignty of kings and queens. So Locke's *Two Treatises of Government*, the second of which contained the material we are interested in, were at first published anonymously.[2]

Locke, like Hobbes, wrote about humanity in the state of nature, but his vision was less apocalyptic. In Locke's worldview, all people were born free and equal, and in the state of nature they would act any way they saw fit within the bounds of what Locke called the law of nature. But he considered it part of this law that no person had power over any other person, and so there would be a natural restraint against subjection and subordination.

The weakness of this law, as Locke saw it, was that it was not written down, and so each person was likely to use it to his or her own advantage without any impartial judge to correct the inevitable abuses.

Ideally, people would be governed by an ethic in which each person had a double duty: first, to claim no property for which he or she had not laboured, and, second, to take only their fair share. To attain this ideal state of affairs, Locke argued, a compact of mutual consent was needed, out of which a government would be created whose function was to provide the greatest happiness for the greatest number. In these words we can hear the pre-figuring of utilitarian theory, which also was to influence the ethics of journalism.

Locke also formulated a statement that was to be echoed in the American Declaration of Independence nearly one hundred years later: 'No one ought to harm another in his life, health, liberty or possessions.'

Locke declared that a government of the sovereign people should guarantee and protect certain individual rights — in particular, the rights of free speech, thought, political belief, and religious worship.

Clearly, then, Locke built on the legacy of Hobbes, but he developed the idea of the social contract much more fully, and introduced into it recognition of what we think of today as basic individual civil rights.

Jean-Jacques Rousseau — born in Geneva in 1712, 33 years after the death of Thomas Hobbes — was to become the philosopher most readily associated today with the idea of the social contract. His book of that name was published in 1762. It began with a statement every bit as famous as any of Hobbes's: 'Man was born free, and everywhere he is in chains.'[3] By this, he meant that individuals had become subservient to the state. At the same time, he argued (as Hobbes did) that might is not right, and that we are obliged to obey only 'legitimate' powers.

He explained the term 'legitimate' this way:

Since no man has natural authority over his fellow, and since strength does not confer right, it follows that the basis remaining for all legitimate authority among men must be agreed convention.

In an echo of Hobbes, Rousseau said:

I make the assumption that there is a point in the development of mankind at which the obstacles to men's self-preservation in the state of nature are too great to be overcome by the strength that any one individual can exert.

Now, as men cannot generate new strength, but only unify and control the forces already existing, the sole means that they still have of preserving themselves is to create, by combination, a totality of forces sufficient to overcome the obstacles resisting them.

The challenge, as Rousseau saw it, was to find a form of association that would defend and protect the life and property of each individual, while preserving the liberty of each individual. In Rousseau's view, 'This is the fundamental problem to which the social contract gives the answer.' Also like Hobbes, Rousseau saw an obligation or a duty on the part of the individual to resist 'physical impulse' and the 'right to appetite' as motivating powers, and instead proclaimed that a person should 'consult his reason before he attends to his inclinations'.

Rousseau went on to talk about the balance of losses and gains for the individual who entered into the social contract: an individual gave up his or her 'natural freedom' and an unlimited right to anything they wanted; in return, they gained civil freedom and the right of property over their possessions. Under this arrangement, the social contract substituted moral and legal equality for whatever degree of physical inequality nature had imposed on people. People might be unequal in physical or intellectual strength, but all enjoyed moral and legal equality through agreed convention and by right.

Rousseau was concerned, however, to strike a balance between the power of the state — as created by what he called the 'general will', which underpinned the social contract — and the liberty of each individual. This concern about individual liberty was the subject of vigorous debate throughout the seventeenth and eighteenth centuries. What were the essential liberties? How might they be preserved? How should the balance be struck between the rights of the individual and the rights of the rest of society?

These questions are central to any consideration of journalism ethics. They arise time and again in the requirements imposed on us to make judgments about whether a private interest outweighs the public interest, or the other way round. They affect decisions we make about what to publish and what to withhold from publication. They go to the heart of what is involved in the ethical exercise of the right of free speech.

The concept of the social contract is also integral to our modern idea of accountability. A leading contemporary political scientist, Robert Behn, argues that 'a compact of mutual, collective responsibility' is the basis for democratic accountability, not in the form of a legal document but as an ethical commitment.[4]

Kantian theory

Immanuel Kant developed what in some respects is a pretty uncompromising interpretation of the obligations we owe each other in keeping our side of the social contract. His moral principles, which he called 'categorical imperatives', published in his *Foundations of the Metaphysics of Morals* in 1785, were based on what he asserted were 'universal laws' — moral rules from which there could be no exception.[5] Perhaps the best known of these is this: 'Act only in accordance with that maxim through which you can at the same time will that it should become a universal law.'

The problem for journalists is that we are called on often to make a decision that requires us to choose between two competing interests, when there is right on both sides. How we make those choices will vary with the circumstances, and this categorical imperative has to be interpreted in a way that makes allowance for that. One way is to think of it as meaning that this is how my ethical dilemma would always be resolved, given the same facts and circumstances.

In another categorical imperative, Kant said, 'Act so that you treat humanity, whether in your own person or in that of another, always as an end and never as a means only.'

This finds many resonances in the ethics of journalism. It entails treating people with respect and, especially, not exploiting them. It is reflected in the values of respect and fairness that underpin the codes. Respect for people means, among other things, that we recognise the autonomy of each individual person. And each person's autonomy is equal to everybody else's — I am not entitled to more autonomy than you are. It is out of the idea of personal autonomy that our concept of individual liberties is born.

So Kant exhorts us not to exploit people, not to disparage or mock them, not to use them for our own advancement or gratification, and not to betray them. In the ethics of journalism, betrayal of the people we write about is one of the most common and difficult problems. We do use people. It is inevitable that this is so. The questions are: Why? To what purpose? And what can we do to minimise it? This is a limitation on the usefulness of Kant for the ethics of journalism, but his rules about exploitation and respect for persons are powerful connectors to the values of the code.

Utilitarian theory

The leading original thinker in the development of utilitarianism was the English lawyer and social reformer Jeremy Bentham. His interests ranged widely across public policy — from prison reform to education, to law and taxation reform. His special contribution to the development of moral philosophy was to separate morality from religion. Morality, he argued, was not about pleasing God, but about acting in ways that added to human happiness here on earth.[6]

This was a radical departure from Western philosophical traditions as they had developed up to that point. Many philosophers — before and since — ground their theories in mankind's relationship with God, humanity's status as a creation of God, and the duties that arise from that status. Bentham proposed instead that the rightness of an action should be judged on the basis of whether it brought about human happiness. In his original formulation, he went further still, saying that a morally right action was one that brought the greatest amount of happiness to the greatest number of people.

However, there is an obvious problem with Bentham's original formulation. Can it be morally right, for example, to inflict misery on one person or on a small number of people for the benefit of a large number of people? Such action might bring happiness to many, but at the cost of causing misery to others. It is in direct conflict with Kant's rule against exploitation and Rousseau's ideal of equality among people.

However, making judgments about the balance between the good of the individual and the good of society is a recurring problem in journalism ethics, because inevitably we find ourselves reporting about one person or a small group of people for the purpose of benefiting a much larger group — our audience, or the public at large. The person or small group who are our subjects have their own legitimate private interests. Our audience or the public at large, on the other hand, may have an interest in knowing this information. Their interest is in receiving this information as members of the public. Theirs is a public, not a private, interest. So we have a balance to strike between the private interests of the person or small group and the public interest of the audience or wider public.

Bentham soon realised that his original formulation — the greatest happiness for the greatest number — was flawed because of this problem. The original formulation implied that some people's interests counted for more than other people's, and this conflicted with the established principle that all human beings should be treated as equals. So he re-formulated it as simply the 'greatest-happiness principle' — that is, the rightness of an action should be judged by the amount of happiness it created.

Utilitarianism was more fully and persuasively developed by John Stuart Mill, a man who was a generation younger than Bentham. Mill expressed Bentham's greatest-happiness principle much more subtly: 'Actions are right in proportion as they tend to promote happiness, wrong as they tend to produce the reverse of happiness.'

Mill defined happiness as 'pleasure and the absence of pain'. He defined unhappiness as 'pain and the privation of pleasure'.[7] Today, we think of these conditions as 'well-being' rather than 'happiness', which has taken on a shallower meaning. The key words in Mill's re-formulation of the greatest-happiness principle are 'proportion' and 'tend'. They remove the absoluteness from the original, and allow us to consider factors other than outright well-being. It means we must make a judgment about the *degree* of well-being that will follow from a moral choice, and the *likelihood* of well-being occurring as a result. In this way, Mill brought into utilitarian theory a responsibility to weigh the negative consequences against the positive consequences of what we do.

Mill also added an element of selflessness — what he called 'impartiality' — to the theory. He did this by asserting that in making moral choices based on utilitarian theory, we are obliged to give our own interests no more and no less weight than we give the interests of everybody else concerned in the matter. We count as one in the utilitarian calculus, and every other person concerned also counts as one.

However, in trying to fix one problem, he created another. Is it humanly possible — never mind right — to be strictly impartial where everyone's well-being is at stake? Don't we put the well-being of our families ahead of others'? Don't we have a responsibility to look after those who are dependent on us directly and personally, before we look after those for whom we have no direct responsibility?

Most of us think we do have such a responsibility: for example, to house, clothe, feed, and educate our own children before doing the same for others. This idea is captured in the everyday phrase, 'Charity begins at home.' So the 'impartiality' element in utilitarian theory, if taken too far, collides with our other responsibilities. Yet useful and relevant aspects of impartiality remain, and of course inform our codes of ethics. A significant part of journalism ethics is concerned with the concept of impartiality.

Another aspect of utilitarian theory that Mill felt it was necessary to clarify was that of intention. He wrote: 'The morality of the action depends entirely upon the intention — that is, upon what the agent wills to do.'

He contrasted this with motive, and it is an important distinction. Our intentions are what we consciously hope will be achieved by our actions. Our motive is why we act as we do. For example, say we publish information that harms someone's reputation. Our intention might be to bring wrongdoing to public attention. Our motive is to stop the wrongdoing; that is what we hope will be achieved. Our motive, then, is to right the wrong, not to harm the wrongdoer, even if that is an unavoidable consequence. If our intention has been simply to harm the individual, we have acted unethically.

Despite Mill's many refinements, the objections to

utilitarianism have never entirely gone away. One of the biggest objections is that utilitarianism looks only at consequences, at what follows from an action.

Mill partly answered this criticism by including a requirement that we treat others as we would want others to treat us, but that doesn't deal with cases where someone is wronged even if they don't know they have been wronged and so suffer no immediate distress.

For example, say a man takes a picture of a woman in a sexually compromising position, and sends it to his friends electronically. The woman is unaware of the fact that her privacy has been grossly violated, so she is not distressed. Yet the fact remains that her privacy has been grossly violated. She has been wronged. Utilitarian theory has nothing to offer us here. In fact, it seems to say that if you can get away with wronging someone without their knowing it, and derive some pleasure from the wrong, it is morally unexceptionable. We know instinctively that this cannot be right. The only way utilitarian reasoning can help us is by reference to the Golden Rule: do unto others as you would have them do unto you.

This has within it the idea of a duty, and it is duty-oriented (deontological) philosophies such as social-contract theory and Kantian ethics that rescues us from this moral dead-end of consequentialist ethics: the social contract is based on a set of unspoken but well-understood mutual obligations, while Kant says we must treat people with respect and not exploit them.

Our codes of ethics have drawn their inspiration from all these traditions of philosophical thought — those from the duties-oriented tradition and those from the consequences-oriented tradition. By way of illustration, we can look at their influence on Australia's only national code, that of the Media,

Entertainment and Arts Alliance, the journalists' professional association and industrial union. The full text of this code is given in the Appendix, but in the table below I have aligned its twelve clauses with the values that govern them. This allows us to look at the values outlined at the start of this chapter, compare them with the values represented in the code, and see the links to the various philosophical traditions.

Values found in codes across the Western world	Philosophical tradition	Relevant clauses of MEAA code
Honesty	Virtue, Social Contract, Kant	1, 8, 9, 10: Honesty
Truth-telling	Virtue, Social Contract, Kant	1, 8, 9: Truth-telling
Fairness	Virtue, Utilitarian	8, 12: Fairness
Respect	Virtue, Social Contract, Kant	2, 8: Respect
Independence	Utilitarian	4, 5, 6: Independence
Confidence-keeping	Virtue, Social Contract, Kant	3: Confidence-keeping
Transparency	Utilitarian	7:Transparency
Responsibility	Virtue	8: Responsibility
Free speech	Social Contract, Utilitarian	*

* While there is no specific clause in the MEAA code dealing with freedom of speech, the associated documentation draws attention to the upholding of free speech as an ethical duty of journalists.

It is not always easy to see straightaway the connections between these abstract concepts and what they mean for the decisions we have to make. The following chapters are designed to help us see how these connections work in a variety of ethical dilemmas. For now, though, it is enough just to summarise how the different philosophical traditions translate into standards of journalism practice.

Virtue

- We act with integrity in all things, in particular by being honest in our dealings with people, and fair in the way we portray them.
- We act responsibly by avoiding doing harm wherever possible, and, where harm is unavoidable, minimising it.

Social Contract

- We have mutual obligations to tell the truth, keep confidences, and keep promises. Without this, the trust that is essential to making the social contract work breaks down. So we place a high price on accuracy and contextual fidelity, and when we receive information in confidence, we keep the promise of confidentiality.
- Might is not right. So we don't use the power of publication to harm or wrong people without good reason.

Kant

- We respect people as human beings by not intruding on their privacy or grief, or by referring to their personal characteristics and beliefs, without good reason.
- We don't exploit people's vulnerability, or take advantage of their ignorance of media practice.
- We recognise people's personal autonomy by obtaining their consent before interviewing or taking images of them, unless there is good reason not to.

Utilitarianism

- We act impartially by not putting one person's interests

ahead of another's, or our own ahead of someone else's. We do this by identifying whose interests and what issues are at stake in a story, and making sure we give them fair and balanced treatment.

- We are transparent about what we do. We don't deceive people. We are open about our own professional processes unless there are good reasons not to be. We avoid or declare conflicts of interest.
- We conduct our journalism independently, free of improper influences and motives.

There is a recurring qualification in these standards — 'good reason'. This is necessary because the professional obligations of journalism sometimes do require us breach these principles and practices: to be covert in our methods; to inflict harm; to intrude; to refer to people's race, religion, gender, or some other personal characteristic; or to not obtain their consent.

A further recurring concept in our decision-making is that of proportionality. Harms we inflict should be proportional to the public-interest considerations being served; standards of proof we require should be proportional to the gravity of the allegations made; and the language we use should be proportional to the subject matter.

At first, these look like a lot of let-outs that weaken our ethical codes. In fact, the reverse is true. They mean that we accept the need to establish ethical bases to justify breaching these standards. This brings with it the need to think through our intentions, motives, and reasons, which requires a moral and intellectual rigour that is not demanded by adherence to absolute rules. Absolute rules require only one thing: obedience. Adherence to our codes requires hard thinking.

FOUR KEY CONCEPTS

Free speech

Four key concepts recur in ethical decision-making for journalism: free speech, the avoidance-of-harm principle, the public interest, and censorship. This chapter discusses each of them. Not all of these concepts are relevant to all decisions, but one or another of them will be present in most cases because ethical decision-making usually means striking a balance that involves at least some of these concepts.

John Locke identified free speech as one of the four basic rights that the people would have to have if they were to be 'the sovereign people'.[1] It is clear why this is so: the people can't be in a position to govern themselves if they can't exchange information, ideas, and opinions; are left in ignorance of what others are thinking or doing; and have no idea of how their society wants to run itself. Moreover, the free exchange of ideas is the means by which knowledge is shared, and the merits of issues decided by reasoned argument. The poet John Milton pressed this case upon the English parliament in 1644, arguing for the abolition of press licensing, a system of censorship in which only those with a licence from the monarch could own a printing foundry or press.[2] Infractions of these laws were dealt with harshly by the Court of Star Chamber.

John Stuart Mill also recognised the central importance of free speech — not just for the purposes of government, but for the general advancement of mankind and the pursuit of truth. It was Mill who wrote a classic case for free speech in his essay *On Liberty*.[3] Importantly for us, he equates freedom of speech with freedom of the press, the press being the only practical means, in his day, by which freedom of speech could be exercised among the population as a whole. The principle still holds today, even if the means of exercising the right of free speech have multiplied.

On Liberty was published in 1859. By this time, the Industrial Revolution had led to the creation of large towns and to the invention of the steam-driven rotary press. These presses were capable of producing something like 24,000 copies of a newspaper an hour — a huge increase on what had been possible with flatbed presses, which printed one page at a time. Also, by this time, compulsory schooling had been introduced, and literacy among ordinary people was expanding rapidly.

The combined effect of these two developments was to increase enormously the potential for people to participate in civic life. Governments are always uneasy when the multitude get ideas in their heads, and the government of Britain was at that very time prosecuting the newspapers for publishing material concerning the lawfulness of the doctrine of tyrannicide. This doctrine held that it was lawful to kill tyrants.

In the circumstances, Mill's chapter on 'Liberty of Thought and Discussion' began boldly: 'The time, it is to be hoped, is gone by when any defence would be necessary of the "liberty of the press" as one of the securities against corrupt or tyrannical government.'

And the core of his argument came shortly thereafter:

If all mankind, minus one, were of one opinion, and only one person were of the contrary opinion, mankind would be no more justified in silencing that one person than he, if he had the power, would be justified in silencing mankind …

The peculiar evil of silencing the expression of an opinion is that it is robbing the human race; posterity as well as the existing generation; those who dissent from the opinion still more than those who hold it. If the opinion is right, they are deprived of the opportunity of exchanging error for truth: if wrong, they lose what is almost as great a benefit, the clearer perception and livelier impression of truth produced by its collision with error.[4]

Mill argued, as Milton had done 200 years earlier when campaigning against press licensing, that truth would emerge from the free exchange of opposing ideas, and that if society wanted to be guided by truth, it had to let this exchange happen. This process acquired the label of 'the marketplace of ideas'.

Vitally important though the value of free speech is, however, it is not an absolute value. Even in the United States, which has perhaps the most highly developed notions of free speech in the world, and has extremely robust protections for it in its laws, freedom of speech is not absolute. There are occasions when it gives way to other values. For example:

- The values of honesty, fairness, and respect mean that people's reputations should not be wrongly trashed.
- The value of justice means that accused people should receive a fair trial based on evidence admitted in court.
- The value that says we owe a duty of care towards children means that it is justifiable to have a system of classification for books, films, and TV programs.

Values-based restrictions on freedom of speech are recognised by the International Covenant on Civil and Political Rights (articles 14, 17, 19, and 20), and have been upheld in a variety of ways by the United States Supreme Court. It has interpreted the First Amendment to the US Bill of Rights — the one that says Congress shall make no law abridging the freedom of the press — in ways that mean different types of speech attract different levels of protection. Political speech is given a very high level of protection, and the concept of political speech is interpreted very broadly. Burning the American flag as an act of protest is regarded as an expression of political speech, and therefore has been protected by the Supreme Court under the First Amendment. Other forms of speech considered to have high social value — scientific speech, which reports scientific debates or findings, and educational speech, which presents all kinds of contending arguments — are also given a high level of protection by the Supreme Court. Commercial speech (advertising, for instance) is given a lower level of protection, because it is judged to be less necessary to the advancement or essential functioning of society.[5]

At the bottom of the list of protected speech come pornographic speech and hate speech (which we in Australia call racial vilification). At this end of the spectrum the balance is struck differently. From balancing the value of the speech against other competing values, freedom of pornographic and hate speech is balanced against the potential harms they might cause.

Australia also has some protections of free speech, although without having available to it anything as sweeping as the First Amendment to the US Constitution. The High Court has construed the Australian Constitution as containing an implied right to freedom of speech on matters of government and politics,[6] and this — along with a public-interest defence

— has since been built into Australia's defamation laws. More generally, Australia has a common-law right to free speech. This means we can speak freely, but we must take the consequences if, in doing so, we breach any law or perpetrate an unjustified wrong on someone. Note, however, that in general there is no *prior* constraint on speech. The exceptions to this usually take the form of a suppression order made by a court, or secrecy provisions in legislation — for example, national security laws. There is considerable debate among media practitioners and lawyers about whether the courts use suppression orders too much or whether there are too many secrecy provisions in the laws, but neither of these can be construed as a general prior constraint on free speech.

The avoidance-of-harm principle

It is fundamental to any system of ethics that we avoid harm where possible, and, where avoidance is impossible, that we minimise it. Medical practitioners take the Hippocratic Oath, one part of which may be summarised as, 'At least do no harm'. Practitioners of journalism cannot be held to that standard if we are to do the job that society expects of us. Inevitably, we will harm people — partly because we are required to expose wrongdoing, and partly because the nature of our work sometimes requires us to deal with people when they are vulnerable or traumatised.

Instead, we are held to a lower standard, but still an important one: if we cannot avoid harm altogether, we must do our best to minimise it. This is a clear ethical duty arising from social-contract, Kantian, and utilitarian principles. In journalism, we have a duty to identify the risk of causing reasonably foreseeable harm. We can call this *anticipated* harm. Risks we cannot reasonably foresee we can call *unanticipated* harm. We also have a duty to honestly examine our motives and intentions. Here we are dealing with what we can call *intentional* and *unintentional* harm. Very often, we will make a decision that will result in *anticipated* but *unintentional* harm. We do this, for example, when we publish a disclosure of wrongdoing by someone. We anticipate that it will harm his or her reputation, but that is neither our motive nor our intention. Our intention is to bring the wrongdoing out into the open; our motives are to put a stop to the wrongdoing and to see justice done.

In these circumstances, harm follows as a by-product of our doing our duty to society. The harm was not intentional, and our motive was not to cause harm, but to do our bit towards setting matters right. Doing *intentional* harm is always unethical. In law, it is called malice, and, as a matter of law, malice defeats certain important legal defences that exist to allow us to report in ways that do cause harm. For example, we may be able to defend on public-interest grounds the defaming of someone, but if a court finds we were actuated by an improper motive, such as revenge or ill will, it will go on to find that we acted out of malice, and the defence will be defeated. It is in this way that the law recognises the difference between unintentional and intentional harm — a distinction that is clearly grounded in ethical principles.

Mill devoted part of his essay *On Liberty* to the exposition of what we call the avoidance-of-harm principle:

> The object of this essay is to assert one very simple principle
> … That the only purpose for which power can be exercised
> over any member of a civilised community, against his will, is
> to prevent harm to others.

And later:

The only freedom which deserves the name is that of pursuing our own good in our own way, so long as we do not attempt to deprive others of theirs.[7]

In journalism, we exercise the power to portray: the power to construct the reality within which the community learns about what is going on. 'Our own good' is generally to be achieved by obtaining and publishing material. That way, we perform our duty to society, fulfil our role in life, advance our careers, and perhaps even attain a certain status. Other people's 'own good', in relation to the work we do as journalists, can take many different forms. On the positive side, they may obtain gratifying publicity for themselves, or some cause or organisation they want to promote. Or they may become the beneficiaries of money raised by the public as a result of what we publish about some disaster they have been caught up in. No ethical difficulties are likely to arise for us in cases where there are positive effects from our work.

On the negative side, however, what we publish might destroy their reputation or their livelihood, or it might embarrass them or show them in a humiliating light, or cause them to feel exploited or exposed in ways that cause them distress.

Sometimes there are both positive and negative effects: they tell their story about how they got caught up in a disaster; their story contributes to an outpouring of public support for themselves and other victims; but the exposure shows them weeping, raw, and at their worst, and they feel deeply hurt by it. We have harmed them. The negative effects of our publishing such material are by definition harmful to people.

Our ethical duty is to do two things. First, we need to ask ourselves whether the good — to the rest of society, to the individual concerned, and to the fulfilment of our role as journalists — outweighs the harm. Second, if we decide that it does, we need to do what we can to minimise the harm.

Harm can be minimised in many ways. We can take pains to ensure that the person understands in advance what kind of story we intend to write. We can be sensitive in the questions we ask. We can be gentle in our demeanour. We can, in cases of personal sensitivity, let our sources see in advance what we have written. We can choose our words in a way that is calculated to be least hurtful. We can frame the story in ways that are less hurtful. We can choose language that is sufficiently strong to make our argument without resorting to gratuitous abuse.

Sometimes — as in the exposure of corruption or serious wrongdoing — the balance can be relatively easy to strike. At other times — as in covering personal tragedy — it can be difficult. One of the most critical and useful ways to strike this balance is to ask ourselves, What is the public interest in this? Does the public interest demand that we inflict this harm, however much we try to minimise it?

Some ethicists also argue that the avoidance-of-harm principle should be applied to the concept of offence: for example, on the grounds that we cause harm by publishing grossly offensive or disturbingly graphic images. [8] Care needs to be taken here, because we are in highly subjective territory. Some people are highly offended by images or words that do not give offence to most people; some people are sickened by images that others find merely necessary to a full understanding of what has happened.

'Offence' is also a criterion in some laws, providing the basis for criminal prosecutions or for civil actions. In Australia, for example, the Racial Discrimination Act makes 'offence' one of four grounds on which a suit for damages may be brought. Section 18C of the act makes it unlawful for a person to perform an act that is 'reasonably likely in all the circumstances, to offend, insult, humiliate or intimidate' someone on grounds of race, colour, nationality, or ethnicity. In 2011, a journalist, Andrew Bolt, and his employer, the Herald and Weekly Times, were successfully sued by an Aboriginal person, Pat Eatock, over articles that disparaged her and a number of other Aboriginal people concerning their appointments to certain positions or their winning of certain grants and awards.[9]

Following this case, there was considerable debate about whether 'offence' and 'insult' were the correct points at which to strike the balance between redress for harm and protection of free speech. The Racial Discrimination Act provides an exemption for anything said or done in good faith in the course of debate on matters of public interest, which is designed as a free-speech defence. However, Bolt was found to have failed the 'good faith' test. Without traversing the rights and wrongs of the case, *Eatock v Bolt* showed how subjective the concept of 'offence' is, and raised the question of whether 'offence' is an appropriate criterion for abridging free speech.

In early 2014, the federal government drafted amendments to the Act, replacing the existing thresholds, including 'offence' and 'insult', with 'vilify' and 'intimidate'. 'Vilify' was defined as inciting hatred, and 'intimidate' was defined as causing fear of physical harm. Under the proposed amendments, the good-faith test would be removed, and the test of whether an act was reasonably likely to vilify or intimidate would be determined by the standards of an ordinary, reasonable member of the Australian community, not the standards of any particular group. These changes went under the name of the *Freedom of Speech (Repeal of S18C) Bill, 2014*.

On the other hand, some material is so gross as to be highly offensive to an ordinary person of reasonable sensibilities. This is what the law calls an objective test, and it is useful also in an ethical context. For example, during the prime ministership of Julia Gillard from 2010 to 2013, depictions of her were published on the Internet in which a photograph of her face was superimposed upon a photograph of a naked woman whose genitals were completely exposed. It was pornographic on any definition of the term, and therefore likely to be highly offensive to an ordinary person of reasonable sensibilities. Moreover, there was no countervailing public interest to be served by publishing the depictions.

The primary harm done by such material is to the dignity of the individual. It also debases public discourse, and contains the risk that it will be seen by children, from whom we screen such images on the ground that they are likely to be psychological harmful. Beyond that, however, applying the avoidance-of-harm principle on the grounds of giving offence begins to trespass on the duty of journalism to engage robustly in informing people and providing a forum for the exchange of ideas. Sometimes offence is given in these robust exchanges, and we need to be careful not to strike the balance in a way that inhibits healthy public debate.

The public interest

'The public interest' is not the same as public curiosity, nor is it assessed by whether a story increases newspaper circulations or generates high levels of online clicks. The public might be interested in or even fascinated by something in the sense that they are curious about it or titillated by it, but that is not what is meant by the term. The public interest means that the public have a substantial and definable stake in a particular matter.

Some people, journalists in particular, equate the public interest with what they call 'the public's right to know'. This is a slippery form of words. It introduces the notion of 'rights', a term properly reserved for entitlements that we tend to think of as being inalienable, as in human rights and civil rights. Entitlement to information is not inalienable; it is contingent. It depends on the nature of the information, the risks and benefits associated with it — as in WikiLeaks — and the balance between the public's interest in having information and the competing interests in, for example, preventing a miscarriage of justice.

A 'right', in this case, is only created by a prior test: what is the public entitled to know, and why? To answer this question, we need to formulate and apply a public-interest test. If we submit our material to such a test and, having balanced the competing considerations, decide that there is a genuine public interest in publishing, we have established an overriding entitlement of the public to know. Then we have a duty to publish. Talking about 'rights' beforehand is getting ahead of ourselves, and is the cause of much bad decision-making by journalists.

Defining the public interest is not easy to do, but there have been many good attempts. Some have defined it as 'the common good', taking into account all relevant considerations. This is a balance of exactly the kind I have been discussing. It requires that we assess each case according to whether, in the circumstances, there is a definable benefit to the public that outweighs any likely harm.

The Herald and Weekly Times, which publishes the *Herald Sun* in Melbourne, once defined it this way in its Professional Practice Policy, although it did not appear in the News Corp code of conduct that superseded it:

> 'Public interest' is defined as involving a matter capable of affecting the people at large so they might be legitimately interested in, or concerned about, what is going on, or what might happen to them or to others.

The key ingredient here is the potential for the matter to have some effect on the public. What kind of effects might this include? A more-or-less standard list has been developed by theorists and practitioners to guide us:

- The existence of crime or serious corruption or impropriety in public life.
- The existence of a threat to public health or safety.
- The existence of a fraud or scam that is likely to mislead or rob the public.
- Exposure of hypocrisy or double standards in public life.
- Betrayal of public trust in something in which the public has a substantial commercial or emotional investment.

The first three are self-explanatory. Note, in the fourth dot point, the introduction of a public-life element. This is important. To satisfy a public-interest test, the hypocrisy or double standards must be indulged in by a public figure and have a bearing on his or her public utterances or duties. It is not enough that the person is a public figure. Public figures are entitled to a private life, and any intrusion on that must be justified on the basis of a public interest proportional to the degree of intrusion.

The fifth point concerns betrayal of the trust the public has placed in a person or organisation that, while not part of our institutional or government arrangements, nonetheless plays an important part in economic or social life. The way public companies conduct themselves is an example of the first. The way a large sporting or cultural organisation conducts itself is an example of the second. For example, in August 2013, the Australian Sports Anti-Doping Authority (ASADA) investigated and reported on the use of performance-enhancing drugs by Australian Football League players at the Essendon club. Australian football is a sport in which many people invest their money and also their passion. This is a relevant interest for the purpose of developing a public-interest test.

Can we distil a good working public-interest test out of all this? The ingredients are integrity in public life, public safety, protection of the public from dishonesty, exposure of failure of public duties by public figures, and protection of public trust where there is a commercial or significant emotional investment. Here is how I conceive of it: the public interest concerns matters that affect public health, safety, or financial security; the capacity of citizens to participate in civic life; or the conduct of affairs in which the public have invested trust.

Two distinguished Australian scholars in this field, Sally White and John Hurst, developed a couple of really useful ways to think about this. They drew a distinction between matters that affect people as citizens (that is, as participants in political, social, and economic life), and those that affect people as individuals with personal tastes and interests.[10]

Matters that affect people as citizens, they classified as information the public 'needs to know'. Matters that affect people as individuals, they classified as information the public might 'want to know'.

None of this is to say journalism does not involve publishing material that the public are curious about — of course it does. However, it is when we reasonably foresee that publication will do harm to others, or depart in any other way from our professional values and standards, that we must apply a public-interest test.

Censorship

Censorship is a dirty word. It has nasty overtones of oppression, and for good reason. Since the dawn of printing, governments of all kinds have tried to control what the public sees and hears through the media. The Tudor and Stuart monarchs of England used the Court of Star Chamber to keep watch on what was printed, and to punish anyone who published 'scandalous reports of persons in power', or promoted the wrong brand of religious belief, or advocated political preferences that did not conform to the monarch's.

The struggle to throw off the yoke of censorship lasted the best part of 250 years, and was gained at the cost of much bloodshed and suffering. This history is imprinted on the DNA of journalism. However, censorship can also be a slippery term. It can be used — and often is — to describe any measure that restricts publication. This is incompatible with certain competing rights, including the right of an individual to have his or her reputation protected from wrongful harm; the right of soldiers not to be imperilled by disclosure of information helpful to the enemy; and the right of people charged with crimes to be tried by due process in the courts and not through the media at the bar of public opinion.

There are laws to control these intersecting rights — laws of defamation, national security, and contempt of court. Our society does not think of these laws as acts of censorship. Why not? After all, they restrict the information that may be published or broadcast. The answer is that society also recognises that the motive for introducing the restriction is a proper one — to prevent unjustified harm to others, and unjustified infringements of their individual rights. Here are echoes again of the social contract and of Mill's avoidance-of-harm principle.

Where the motive for restricting or preventing publication is an *improper* one — to prevent embarrassment to the government, silence a dissenting opinion, or suppress ideas because they challenge existing wisdom — we have censorship.

Motive is the central consideration here. Before jumping to the view that any restriction on publication is censorship, we should ask why the restriction is being imposed, and then assess whether it is defensible as a proper motive or indefensible as an improper one.

This matters to any individual who practises journalism, because we are called upon every day to make decisions about what to publish and what not to. Every available fact that we leave out of a story is an act of … what? Censorship? Hardly. To judge whether we are engaging in an act of censorship (or self-censorship, as some practitioners call it), we need to ask ourselves these questions:

1. Is this fact essential to my audience's getting a full understanding of the story?
2. By leaving out this fact, am I skewing the story so that it will give a different impression from what would be given if I put it in?
3. Am I covering up anything?
4. Why am I leaving this out? What are my motives and intentions?

For example, in reporting the Black Saturday bushfires in Victoria in February 2009, many journalists left out material that contained gruesome details about how people died or the state of their bodies when found. Many of them spoke of this as 'self-censorship'. Yet they went on to give sound ethical reasons for excluding this material: to spare the feelings of family members and survivors; to spare the sensibilities of the public at large; and to preserve the dignity of the dead.

This is a good example of the difference between editing and censorship: the motives behind the decision. Was the material being withheld in order to deny the public information they needed to know, or to prevent embarrassment to some person or organisation? Many journalists who covered the fires used the 'need to know' test when deciding how much grisly detail to put in their copy — and the answer tended to be 'none' or 'not much'. They asked themselves: can I tell the story without putting this in? For example, it was considered sufficient to say that a man died in his utility truck while trying to outrun the fire. It did not add to the public's understanding of what had happened for the reporter to add detail about the condition of the body.

Making assessments about what the public needed to know, and balancing that against the risk of harm to individuals, was particularly complex in the WikiLeaks cases of 2010, discussed in chapter one. At one level, these assessments were quite straightforward: if the matter was clearly a matter of public interest, and the only harm would be to embarrass the United States or some other government, the decision to publish was relatively easy. However, some of the material contained names of informers and spies in the war zones of Afghanistan and Iraq, and if these names were to be published there was a substantial risk that the individuals would be killed, and perhaps other reprisals taken.

Removal of material simply because it might embarrass a government would unequivocally constitute censorship, because it is an improper motive for suppressing information. Removing it to preserve people's lives is not censorship, because the motive for suppressing the information is a proper one. It arises from an ethical obligation to balance risk with benefit. When the risk is to life, it will be rare that a benefit overrides it.

CHAPTER FIVE
IMPARTIALITY

Impartiality is the quality of giving all relevant people and interests equal *consideration* — not necessarily equal *treatment*. It also entails not putting our own interests ahead of other people's. As it happens, the idea that journalists should be impartial in their reporting of the news is relatively recent: it really only took hold in the West in the early twentieth century, and was given particular status after the United States Commission on the Freedom of the Press produced a highly influential report in 1947 on how the press should conduct itself.

The commission was established and paid for by the publishing industry — specifically Time Inc and the *Encyclopaedia Britannica* — because of the industry's concern that its poor reputation was having adverse commercial repercussions. There were no journalists or publishers on the commission, and it was composed entirely of distinguished men from public life. It was chaired by the chancellor of the University of Chicago, and its most influential member was a Harvard philosopher, William Ernest Hocking, who wrote a companion volume to the main report.[1]

This report laid the foundations for what has come to be called the Social Responsibility theory of the press — which, broadly speaking, is the theory that still guides the practice of journalism in Western democracies today. The theory proclaims, basically, that in return for certain privileges and freedoms, the press will discharge certain functions, such as providing information, being a forum for debate, and being a watchdog on those in power.

One of the important ideas in the commission's report was that comment, or opinion, should be separated from the reporting of the news — reporting should just be about providing the facts. We would extend that nowadays to say that reporting is also about explaining the facts and helping the audience make sense of them. But we would retain the essence of the principle: this should be done in a way that minimises the intrusion of our own value judgments about whether, for example, the subject of our report is good or bad, should be supported or opposed, and is desirable or undesirable.

The intrusion of opinion into news reporting — often in the form of political propaganda or promotion of the newspaper owner's self-interest — was one of the sources of the public dissatisfaction with the media that had caused the sponsors of the commission such concern. Material that was meant to be news was mashed up with the preferences and prejudices of either the reporter or the editor or, most likely, the proprietor. The community was being robbed of reliable information it needed in order to know, understand, and make up its own mind about what was going on in the world. There are many parallels between this type of so-called journalism and the type that is burgeoning today on the Internet: a mélange of reportage, gossip, rumour, and opinion — some written in good faith, some in bad.

As a result of the US commission's report, impartiality became a high value in the profession of journalism. Comments or opinions were taken out of the news pages of newspapers, and inserted in pages set aside for the purpose — what came to be called the leader or editorial page and the 'op ed' page, the page opposite the editorial page. These pages contained the paper's own opinion in the form of editorials, and other people's opinions in the form of cartoons, letters to the editor, and signed columns or argumentative articles. News pages were to be free from comment or, if comment were to appear, it was to be labelled as such. News reporting was expected to be impartial, objective, value-free.

For much of the twentieth century the ideal of impartiality was expressed through the term 'objectivity'. This was a method, a set of rules, for enforcing detachment by the reporter from any inclination to interpret, analyse, or explain, much less make value judgments. Reporters reported the facts, and nothing more. As the ethicist Stephen Ward put it, 'The traditional language of journalistic objectivity was a language of self-denial, restraint, and exclusion.'[2]

Over the latter half of the twentieth century, the limitations imposed by this method were beginning to chafe against the capacity of journalism to properly perform its function of informing the public. Practitioners and scholars realised that audiences needed more than just bare facts: they needed explanation and context. Today, we go further still and say the public needs analysis, and, in the digital age, some evaluation of what is credible. On top of that, 'objectivity' was seen as a sham because it denied the reality that all reporters, no matter how conscientious, brought to their work their own background, values, beliefs, and attitudes from which they could not separate themselves and which therefore, in the nature of things, influenced their work. These challenges gathered strength until, by the turn of the millennium, 'objectivity' had been abandoned in favour of notions of truth-telling and fairness.

Unfortunately, the ideal of impartiality suffered some collateral damage, as it became conflated with objectivity.

Practitioners took refuge in the truism that bias is in the eye of the beholder. Of course, there is some truth in this: people commonly do allege bias when the content or presentation of a story does not conform to their own view. But to just leave it there is to accept that there is no way to assess impartiality. In fact, there is a way, and it starts by breaking impartiality down into its constituent elements.

Elements of impartiality

It has been demonstrated experimentally that impartiality in journalism has six core elements: accuracy, fairness, balance, freedom from conflict of interest, open-mindedness, and decision-making based on news values.[3]

Accuracy

Facts must not only be correctly stated, but put together in a way that gives an honest overall impression of the subject of a story. This is called contextual accuracy. It is more familiar to think about this in the negative, as when people say that something has been 'taken out of context'. This usually means that while the facts as reported are not in dispute, they have been presented in a way that gives a false or misleading impression. For example, a story reporting that principals of private schools had expressed concern about the rate of increase in school fees would take on a different hue if it included the fact that their concerns were stated in a submission to the federal government for an increase in government assistance. Their position would change from what might look like concern for the welfare of families to what was, in fact, a request to the government for more money.

Accuracy depends on verification, which is the subject of chapter nine. We must check our evidence until we are satisfied that it is the best available version of the truth. An important aspect of verification arises from the use of websites as sources, and of hyperlinks, where we might send our readers for further material. One test of our impartiality is whether we have satisfied ourselves that they are reliable. Another test is whether we create hyperlinks only to sites that contain information we agree with, or to those that reflect other important and relevant perspectives on an issue.

Fairness

There are many facets to fairness in the practice of journalism. At the outset, the people being reported on are entitled to know that they are going to be the subject of a story and, so far as it is known at the time, the nature of the story. This is particularly the case in circumstances where the people being reported on are not likely to be familiar with journalistic practice, or where they are distressed or otherwise vulnerable. This is related to the issue of consent, which is the subject of chapter eight.

As to content, the concept of fairness is captured in the well-worn phrase 'telling all sides of the story'. This does not necessarily mean giving equal weight to all sides, as we will see when I discuss the notion of balance.

However, to ignore or exclude the contribution of a party to the story is to imperil the fairness of the story. Whether, in fact, this results in unfairness depends on the salience of the party's contribution or on whether the excluded party is denied what is commonly called 'the right of reply'. This should be thought of not as a legal right, but as an ethical right.

A third facet of fairness concerns the presentation of story subjects. A useful test is to ask onself, *Would I like to be portrayed like this?* If the answer is no, the next question is, *What is the justification for my portraying the subject this way?*

If the justification is not proportional to the harm contained in the portrayal, the portrayal is ethically unjustifiable.

A fourth facet of fairness concerns the labelling of groups or individuals. It is ethically unjustified to do so except where such labels provide essential information or context. The characteristics to which reference should be avoided, unless they are relevant, include race; ethnicity; nationality; sex; age; disability; sexual preference; marital, parental, social or occupational status; religious, cultural, or political belief or activity; and physical characteristics.

A fifth facet of fairness concerns verification. Failure to take adequate steps to verify material results not only in a failure of accuracy but a failure of fairness. It suggests indifference to the consequences of publication for the subject of the story and for the publisher.

Balance

Balance is a different concept from fairness. It concerns the extent to which coverage of an issue comprehends and evaluates all the main perspectives. How it is assessed may vary.

During election campaigns, for example, it is usually assessed quantitatively by measuring how much time, space, and relative prominence is given to the political parties contesting the election. While these kinds of data are useful, they are not usually sufficient. The nature of the content is also an important factor. For example, Candidate A gets 10 minutes, during which he is asked a few soft questions and is otherwise allowed to give an unchallenged spiel. Then Candidate B gets 10 minutes, during which she is subjected to a rigorous cross-examination, conducted in a hostile and disbelieving tone. They both get 10 minutes of airtime, but their treatment is hardly equivalent.

This is the stuff of content analysis, and is commonly assessed quantitatively by reference to a scheme of categorisation leading to a calculation about whether a particular story was positive, negative, or neutral from the perspective of some identified party. In addition, balance is usually assessed qualitatively by reference to factors such as tone, style of questioning, interruptions, and the nature of the opportunity to be heard — which is really about program format (such as chat show, news bulletin, current-affairs program, or feature).

Another aspect of balance is proportionality. We should use language that is proportional to the facts: not every misfortune is a tragedy; not every survivor is a hero; not every criticism is an attack.

Most important of all, balance follows the weight of evidence. Balance is not achieved merely by giving all parties equal time or space without regard for the state of knowledge about the subject. Failure to do so is irresponsible. For example, there is a small but vocal minority of people who say — in the face of clear scientific evidence to the contrary — that the risk of immunising children against preventable disease is greater than the risks from the diseases themselves. To simply report this assertion alongside an assertion to the contrary by an immunologist, as if the two assertions were of equivalent scientific value, is a failure of balance. This is a common failure in journalism, and in a case like this it can have serious consequences for community health.

It is one of the professional responsibilities of journalism to become sufficiently well acquainted with the evidence to be able to make an informed evaluation of it, and to arrive at a decision that follows the weight of evidence.

No conflicts

The basic rule is that if a journalist has any kind of material interest — financial, familial, associational — in the subject matter of a story, this should be disclosed and, if possible, avoided. If it is unavoidable, the interest should be disclosed with the story. A particular difficulty arises when a journalist becomes a participant in a story. Participation in this sense means that the journalist figures as part of the story beyond being simply the reporter or editor of it. The journalist's participation might bestow certain advantages of a professional nature on any organisation he or she works for because of the special knowledge or connections the participation might bring. But this is counter-balanced by the inevitable perception, justified or not, that the journalist's coverage lacks professional detachment.

It is probable that the coverage will affect the journalist personally. His or her personal honour or professional reputation might be at stake, or the impact of publicity itself might have an effect simply because it may generate notoriety and an unfamiliar type of public recognition. It is this that creates the potential for a conflict between the journalist's personal interests and professional responsibilities. In such cases, disclosure of the interest is not usually going to be a sufficient remedy, because it neither removes the perception problems nor the problems that may arise from the personal impact of the story on the journalist.

The only real solution here is to remove the journalist from reporting the story, and to treat him or her as a participant instead, leaving the reporting of it to someone else. This is precisely what did not occur in 2007, when three senior reporters in the Canberra press gallery became embroiled in a controversy with the then treasurer of Australia, Peter Costello, over whether a particular story was right or wrong.

In 2005, the three reporters — one from the ABC and two from *The Bulletin* — had dined with Costello and one of his advisers. In August 2007, *The Bulletin* published a story based on a conversation at the dinner during which, it reported, Costello had questioned whether the government of which he was part could win the forthcoming election while John Howard remained as prime minister. Costello denied this, and speculated about the reliability of journalists generally. The other two journalists — the ABC's and the other *Bulletin* reporter, who was by now working for *The Age* — corroborated their colleague's story.

The matter was further complicated by the fact that there was a dispute between Costello and his adviser on the one hand, and the journalists on the other, about the status of the conversation: whether it was 'off the record' or 'on background' (see chapter ten).

There had been long-running leadership tensions between Costello and Howard, so this was a major political story. On top of that, there was now a question about Costello's credibility — a question in respect of which each of the reporters was, in effect, a witness.

At the ABC, there was a subsequent internal inquiry into the way this story was handled, and a report about it was published.[4] The reporter involved had been permitted to continue reporting the story, and his role had been clearly declared. There was no evidence that he misreported or distorted his coverage, but the perception of a conflict of interest was ineradicable. The inquiry found that, in retrospect, he should have been taken off the story and treated as a participant. There is no evidence, incidentally, that any such soul-searching occurred at the other two outlets.

The ABC report made the point that, in cases such as this, mere disclosure of the conflict of interest is of limited use. It went on:

The journalist's involvement in such situations may be well known, and it may heighten the perception that independence is in question. Typical phrases from the language encapsulate the issue. We sometimes say a person is 'too close', 'can't stand back from it', 'hasn't got the distance', or 'has lost perspective'.

Open-mindedness

Open-mindedness entails going into a story without a pre-conceived idea of how it should turn out, regardless of the evidence. It also means avoiding conscious prejudice or consciously giving weight to personal feelings, convictions, or preferences in a way that promotes or retards particular interests. An example of such prejudice arose in the late 1970s, when the foreign-affairs correspondent of a capital-city daily newspaper in Australia took a personal dislike to a very senior government official. Many of the correspondent's articles were refracted through the prism of this dislike, which led eventually to a successful action for defamation by the official against the newspaper. The evidence of personal animus was part of the basis for a judgment that the journalist had been actuated by malice. This led to aggravated damages being awarded against the newspaper.

Decisions based on news values

News values are not simply a journalist's gut instinct for what makes a story. Journalism's professional literature offers a substantial body of ideas about what constitutes 'news', and there is a reasonably high degree of consensus about it.[5] The news values that matter most for our purposes are these:

News value	What it means
Magnitude	The size or scale of an event and its impact. Examples: the 11 September 2001 attacks on New York and Washington; the 2004 Boxing Day tsunami in Asia.
Timeliness/ Continuity	The newness or recency of an event or development, especially in relation to an outlet's production deadlines; the continued unfolding of a story that has already become established.

Proximity	This has two dimensions.
	    Geographic proximity means that a story geographically close to home is bigger than the same thing happening further away. Example: an earthquake in Newcastle where eight people are killed is a bigger story in Australia than an earthquake in Chile where 100 people are killed.
	    Cultural proximity means that a story happening to 'people like us' or with whom we identify is a bigger story than the same thing happening to people with whom we, as a society, are not familiar. Example: in Australia, a bomb on the London Underground in 2005 was a bigger story than a bomb on the Madrid railway in 2004, even though the death toll in Madrid was three times greater.

Consequence	Sometimes called 'significance', this concerns the extent to which an event affects our society. Example: the High Court's judgment on native title in the Mabo case. This obliterated the doctrine of terra nullius, altering one of the fundaments of the white settlement of Australia, and conferring new legal rights on Australia's indigenous people.

News value	What it means
Unexpectedness	This has two dimensions, shock and novelty. Shock: the killing of a man going to the assistance of a woman in peak hour in Melbourne's CBD. Novelty: Unusual stories, such as shark or crocodile attacks on people.
Conflict	One of the most pervasive news values, this concerns any kind of argument or controversy, as well as violence.
Human interest	This concerns stories that say something universal, poignant, inspiring, or tragic about the human condition, usually from the experiences of one person or a small group of people.

Fame	This has three dimensions: celebrity, authority, and prominence.
	  Celebrity at its most banal is the Paris Hilton syndrome, whereby a person is famous for being famous. However, it has substance when allied to excellence of achievement as with sporting, artistic, cultural, and scientific celebrities.
	  Authority is related to a person's position or status. It may be conferred by formal office (the prime ministership); by recognised moral leadership (Sir William Deane as governor-general); or by expertise (the Nobel laureate Peter Doherty).
	  Prominence derives from being highly visible or influential, and not necessarily for positive reasons.

Negativity	Bad news nearly always outranks good news.
Clarity	A simple story where good and evil are in stark contrast is a bigger story than a complex one where the rights and wrongs may not be clear.
Consonance	A story that reinforces what we already know and is consonant with our existing view of the world is a bigger story than one that challenges this view.

Part of any judgment about impartiality is the extent to which a story contains any of these news values. To not publish a story that contains at least some of these news values is to invite a question about suppression; to publish a story that contains none of them is to invite a question about undue prominence.

This impartiality matrix was tested experimentally by the ABC in 2007, and its use was found to help distinguish between impartial and biased coverage of a specific controversial issue — the deepening of the shipping channel in Port Phillip Bay, Melbourne. The coverage by three media outlets was assessed: the *Herald Sun*'s, *The Age*'s, and the ABC's. Use of the matrix resulted in an assessment that the coverage by the *Herald Sun* and the ABC had been impartial, but that the coverage by *The Age* had been biased. Coincidentally — and after the findings had been written, though not published — the editorial staff of *The Age* held a stop-work meeting to protest at what they said was the biased coverage of the issue by their own newspaper. They said the editor was running an 'undeclared campaign' against the channel-deepening, and that this had compromised the news reporting of the issue. The cause of the bias was a matter of speculation among editorial staff, but there was no explanation of it from the editor.

The heartening lesson from this experience is that a discussion about impartiality does not need to stop abruptly with the all-purpose declaration that bias is in the eye of the beholder. For professional purposes, we do have a way of assessing our performance. As the digital information revolution matures, it is likely that the community will demand higher standards of impartiality from online journalism than it now gets, and that as a result impartiality will be part of the critical distinction between what is recognised as journalism and what is dismissed as something else.

CHAPTER SIX
CONFLICT OF INTEREST

The polar opposite of impartiality occurs when a conflict of interest arises. Here is a definition of this concept drawn from an Australian Broadcasting Corporation seminar on the topic, so it is apt for journalism: 'A conflict of interest is a real or seeming incompatibility between a person's duty and his or her private interests.'

Other authorities offer variants on this definition. Edward Wasserman proposes this:

> Conflict of interest comprises a variety of instances where undeclared obligations or loyalties exist that might plausibly intervene between journalists and journalism organisations and the public they principally serve.[1]

It can be seen that Wasserman imports three characteristics:

1. Lack of disclosure ('undeclared obligations or loyalties').
2. Plausibility (in the sense that there is some rational basis for thinking a conflict might occur).
3. An organisational as well as individual dimension.

This also is an area in which perceptions matter. The Media, Entertainment and Arts Alliance Code of Ethics captures this where it asks its members to disclose 'conflicts of interest that affect, or could be seen to affect, the accuracy, fairness or independence of your journalism'.

This clause also emphasises disclosure, and does so in a way that invites the inference that disclosure is a sufficient remedy. In reality, disclosure may not always be a sufficient remedy, although it will usually help.

Stephen Tanner, an Australian media ethicist, has identified three levels at which conflicts of interest can occur in the media:

1. Institutional (arising from potential conflicts between the business and editorial sides of media organisations).
2. Process (which might include chequebook journalism, the potential for conflicts inherent in the rounds system such as 'capture', and the effect of policies concerning free travel or other goods and services about which the journalists concerned publish material).
3. Personal (individual journalists' interests or loyalties).[2]

It can be seen that the notion of 'competing loyalties' is a useful way to help identify a conflict of interest. It also helps by drawing attention to the multiple and sometimes conflicting loyalties to which a journalist may be bound. It can also be seen that a conflict of interest can and does arise frequently. For example, a reporter who declines to publish newsworthy material because it may cause justifiable harm to a valued contact has succumbed to a conflict of interest. In doing so, the journalist also exhibits symptoms of what is called 'capture', of having become so reliant on a particular source for information that he or she has become captive to it. This is a very common problem, and one of the big recurring challenges for those who manage newsrooms.

Matters concerning the separation of the editorial and commercial sides of a media business are usually the province of editors, but they can also affect ordinary working journalists, too — such as the TV-guide editor who is showered with the latest electronic gadgetry, or the travel editor who gets a free trip every other week. Some organisations have policies for these. The code of conduct for News Corp, for example, states that any gift valued at more than $100 must be declared.

Newspapers also generally require that a footnote be added to any story declaring any relevant financial interest by the reporter. In addition, in some newspapers, editorial executives are required to make a written declaration of their financial affairs to the editor. These are generally not able to be checked because of privacy laws, but it is understood that failure to disclose is a sacking offence.

Real estate presents special challenges. In the early 2000s, at a suburban newspaper chain in Sydney, a young journalist, quite new to the paper and relatively inexperienced, was made editor of the real-estate section. This meant she had to look at the properties listed in the paper for sale each week, and choose one to write about, with pictures, on the front cover of the real-estate section. In its own small way, this was a quite powerful prerogative: extra publicity of this kind would obviously be very valuable to the person selling the featured property, since it was considered axiomatic that the material would be favourable.

She soon discovered that some of the advertising-sales staff were usurping her editorial right to make this choice by promising front-cover treatment to especially valued real-estate agents. What should she do? She was troubled that editorial decisions were being taken out of the hands of editorial staff. She was further troubled by discovering that some of the newspaper's advertising-sales staff were moonlighting for certain real-estate agents at weekends, acting as sales staff for them as well. She clearly and rightly saw this not only as a conflict of interest for them, but for the paper, too. If it got out that some of the newspaper's staff were working privately for some agencies, the paper's relationship with the rest of the industry would be seriously compromised.

Moreover, she suspected, but could not prove, that the people making the improper promises of front-cover treatment were also involved in the moonlighting, and were making these promises to the firms for whom they were doing the moonlighting. She sat on all this for months, stewing about what to do, and then, at a staff seminar on ethics conducted by someone from outside the company, took the opportunity to bring it all out. She subsequently reported the matter to her supervisor. It is not known what action, if any, the supervisor took.

The potential for conflicts of interest between the editorial and commercial sides of big media companies has long been recognised; as a result, many companies kept a clear separation between the commercial side of the business, which was focused on selling advertising, and the editorial side, which was focused on news. In some companies, this was rather grandly referred to as the separation of church and state. Conceited though it sounds, it did symbolise a genuine and substantive independence of the editorial side from the commercial considerations of the company. If a news story was bad for a big advertiser, so be it. If a news story was good for a big advertiser, steps were taken to ensure that the news story did not appear anywhere near an advertisement for that company.

And in the Fairfax company, at least, the church-and-state separation went further still. There, the editor's prerogative extended to challenging advertising content if it contained material of relevance to an existing news story. In the late 1970s, for example, a large mining company wanted to run a full-page advertisement in *The Sydney Morning Herald* to rebut allegations that had been made against it in a television current-affairs program. The text of the proposed advertisement also contained an attack on the professional integrity of the journalists and television station that had broadcast the program. The editor refused to publish it, saying it was defamatory of the journalists. The mining company offered to indemnify the newspaper against any legal liability arising from an action for defamation, but the editor once more refused, saying he was not prepared on principle to publish such an attack from a partisan interest without the journalists and television station having the opportunity to respond. The editor's stand was supported by the company management, and the advertisement did not run.

In some media organisations, this separation of editorial from commercial interests was enshrined in charters of editorial independence. The critical element of such charters was that the editor had full control of the editorial budget and the editorial space. These were always subject to negotiation; but, once the amount had been fixed, it was the editor's prerogative to decide how they should be used. This meant it was the editor who would decide how many journalists to employ, on what salaries, and for what purposes. He would also decide how to deploy them, and what stories to assign to them. It also meant that once the editorial space for the day's paper had been settled — and this was a function of the ratio of advertising to editorial — it was for the editor to decide what content to put in, what to leave out, and what prominence it should have. In practice, of course, many of these decisions were delegated to other editorial executives, but the editor had the final say.

This did not mean that the editor was immune from commercial or political pressure. In fact, these pressures were constant. It was how he or she responded to this pressure that defined the quality of the editorship. Where the editorial culture was strong, resistance to pressure was also strong, and it tended to permeate all levels of the editorial staff. This, in turn, tended to breed strong editors who sustained the culture.

On the other hand, where the editorial culture was weak, the separation of editorial from commercial content broke down. In one notorious series of cases, the people involved in creating the editorial content became complicit in the breakdown for personal financial gain. These became known as the cash-for-comment cases, which involved five commercial talkback radio presenters who, in 1999–2000, were subjected to an inquiry by the Australian Broadcasting Authority, which was at that time the broadcasting regulator. The inquiry found that the five presenters had entered into commercial agreements with program sponsors to promote their goods and services in the guise of editorial comment or opinion. In return, the presenters would receive financial remuneration. This led to the creation of three new standards for commercial broadcasters concerning disclosure of agreements between sponsors and presenters. And in the United States, so-called 'payola' laws were introduced as a deterrent to similar agreements there.

So the conflict-of-interest terrain was a pockmarked battlefield well before the digital revolution. What the revolution has brought, however, is a structural change in which editorial–commercial conflicts are now openly built in to media advertising arrangements. And this phenomenon even has its own jargon.

The new landscape was surveyed by the ABC-TV program *Media Watch* on 22 July 2013. The program began by noting that two commercial television channels were emerging from a period of only marginal solvency, and that newspaper advertising revenue was down 20 per cent on the previous year's. As the presenter, Paul Barry, put it, 'Everyone is desperate for revenue, and eager to give advertisers whatever they want.'

The program then presented a number of case studies illustrating the radical erosion of the separation between commercial and editorial sides of media companies that had occurred in the space of only about eight years — so desperate had the struggle for financial survival become.

In one case study, a commercial television station broadcast what looked like its nightly news bulletin — using its channel logo, its news set, and its news presenter, who conducted what appeared to be an interview with someone who appeared to be a financial expert about a cut in interest rates that had just occurred. In fact, this was an elaborate advertisement for a mortgage finance company, whose logo also appeared with the channel's own logo on the opening slide, and the company was named when the interviewee was introduced.

The jargon term for this kind of fake news is 'sponsored segments'. *Media Watch* called it 'prostitution'. Others — and not just the television channel — responded by saying that this was now simply the way of the world, and that calling it prostitution was naïve.

There were other jargon terms, too, for other varieties of this phenomenon: 'branded content' and 'content integration' were two of them. News Corp, which controlled 70 per cent of Australia's daily newspaper circulation, used these terms in presentational material for advertising-sales purposes. It defined 'branded content' as occurring when the newspaper company 'commissions journalists to write content which reflects the brand attributes and values of the advertiser'. It defined 'content integration' as occurring when 'existing content relevant to an advertiser is sponsored or branded for a period of time'.

If this was what some of the big media companies were having to do to stay afloat, what did it say about the financial challenges facing online journalism start-ups? Money was usually short. Opportunities might arise for advertising or other forms of revenue to be obtained in return for product endorsement, or at least a favourable article. The pressure could be acute.

The risk — to the established companies as well as to the start-ups — was that their editorial content would not be trusted by the audience to be free of taint by commercial interests. If consumers couldn't trust the editorial content, why would they read it? And if no one read it, why would anyone advertise in it?

Solutions to this are difficult. It is possible that transparency will work, at least some of the time. A clear statement or declaration that there is a sponsor for an article, or a feature, or a page may help. Some broad declaration of policy, saying that editorial decision-making is made independently of advertising interests, might work — so long as it is adhered to. A general approach to presentation that clearly distinguishes between editorial and advertising content may also help. Declarations of individual interest — say, where a writer belongs to an organisation whose cause he or she is championing — would help, too.

The bottom line is likely to be something like this: where people can distinguish between news and commercial content, even when there is clearly a commercial connection, they are likely to be tolerant, so long as the content interests them. What is unlikely to work in the long run is deceit — advertisements masquerading as news, or so-called news stories that are nothing more than disguised product endorsements.

CHAPTER SEVEN
'THE GRINDER'

In 2013, a group of commercial television news and current-affairs executives in Melbourne sat around a table discussing the complexities of ethical decision-making. They were serious, intelligent, tough-minded professionals looking for ways to do their job better. Some way into the discussion, after several difficult issues such as chequebook journalism, standards of proof, and intrusions on privacy and grief had been canvassed, one of them said: 'You know what? We need some kind of grinder, some kind of mechanism, to help us think through these things.'

This chapter describes just such a 'grinder', and illustrates how it works. It isn't the only way, but it is *one* way to think through what can be really complex decisions. It is a modified version of a model for systematically thinking about moral reasoning called the Potter Box, named after an American academic, Professor Ralph Potter of Harvard Divinity School, who developed it in the late 1950s and early 1960s to help him and other theologians think about how a Christian society should respond to the ethical issues presented by the nuclear bomb.

However, it is not a religious tool. It is a thoroughly secular tool, based not on Christian or other religious principles, but on moral principles of the kind we have found already in virtue theory, social-contract theory, Kantian ethics, and utilitarianism, and it can allow us to apply important concepts such as the avoidance-of-harm principle and the public-interest standard.

The original model was not designed for the particular requirements of journalism ethics, so what I offer here is a modified version that is more useful for our purposes. Before we get to the adaptation, however, here is a description of the original.

The Potter Box has four quadrants.

The first quadrant (top left) is called *Situation* or *Situational Definitions*. This is where we define the situation by putting in the basic facts that form the case we have to decide. Doing this also helps us to start thinking about the values, principles, interests, and loyalties that we are going to have to consider in arriving at our decision.

The second quadrant (bottom left) is called *Values*. In this box we write the values we think are relevant to the decision we have to make. Usually, because we are journalists, one of those values will be the value of free speech, but it will not be the only one. Filling in this quadrant requires us to be intellectually honest and to recognise values that may compete with the free-speech value.

The third quadrant (bottom right) is called *Principles*. In this quadrant we identify the ethical rules governed by the values we have already identified. If we have identified, say, confidence-keeping and respect (say, for someone's privacy) as the relevant values, then in the Principles quadrant we are going to have two statements. One will say something like, 'When we receive a confidence, we keep it.' The other will say something like, 'We don't intrude on a person's privacy without good reason.'

The fourth quadrant (upper right) is called *Loyalties*. Here we identify those to whom we owe loyalties in the matter, and prioritise them. Like Quadrant Two, where we identified the values we think are relevant, in filling in Quadrant Four we need to be intellectually honest. It is very easy to be self-serving about this. We might say out loud that we owe our first loyalty to our audience, but deep down we know that, in fact, we put loyalty to our own career ahead of everything else.

Now for the adaptation. I propose that we need to take account of one further set of factors: interests. Whose interests are at stake here, and how should they be prioritised? This helps to clarify the question of loyalties.

So the modified box has five segments:

1. The factual situation.
2. The values that the factual situation calls on us to consider.
3. The principles governed by those values.
4. The interests at stake.
5. The loyalties we owe.

There aren't any hiding places with the box. It demands that we be explicit and up-front about why we decide to do what we do. We can fool ourselves if we want to, but the box has a way of reflecting that back at us like a mirror.

Applying the modified box

Let us apply the modified box now to a real case. The scenario goes like this: You are a reporter covering a major bushfire in which many people have died and several towns have been destroyed. You find yourself, the day after, outside the fire station of a small settlement that was spared. It is about two o'clock in the afternoon.

You see a large crowd of 200 or 300 people gathered around outside the fire station. They seem animated, excited, laughing. This strikes you as perhaps even a bit hysterical; it certainly seems bizarre. On the morning after a dreadful tragedy in which many people are known to have died, here these people are, laughing and seemingly exuberant. Are they heartless, oblivious to other people's suffering, or is there something else going on here?

You talk to a few people, but you don't get much out of them. They're glad to be alive — that's about all they can say to you. They're waiting to hear about friends and relatives. They're a bit anxious, but they're hoping for the best. They're pre-occupied. They don't want to give interviews, and anyway it's all too rowdy to do a useful interview.

You aren't a psychologist. You have no training in making assessments about whether people are in shock or traumatised, and this behaviour really troubles you. You can't understand it. You ask yourself, *How can I convey this to my audience in a way that will make sense to them, when I can't make sense of it myself?*

Just then, the captain of the local fire brigade comes over. He tells you that these people are waiting to hear about what happened to their friends and relatives in a nearby town that has been totally destroyed. He goes on to tell you that the police will arrive shortly, bearing the dreadful news that there have been no survivors in that town. Anyone who was there when the fire struck is dead.

He asks you to back off, to give the people some privacy, as they hear this appalling news.

You think — although you do not know — that you and your photographer are the only media people present. You both retreat to the far side of the football oval, from where you can see what happens.

The police arrive and make their announcement.

Immediately the crowd wilts. People fall into each other's arms. One young man comes running out into the middle of the oval, where he sits and rocks and howls like a wild animal. After a time, someone comes and takes him by the shoulders and leads him away. At length, the crowd breaks up and the people drift off. You are left to decide what, if anything, you will publish about these events.

Let us now apply the modified box to this scenario.

Segment 1: Situation

You need to assess the relevance of the facts that:

- In the immediate aftermath of the fire, a large crowd of people are behaving in a way that is bizarre and inexplicably exuberant.
- Within a short time, however, they are bereaved. Some show their grief graphically, oblivious to the fact that they are in public.
- You have been specifically asked to respect their privacy in their hour of grief.
- You have seen but not recorded any of this in writing, on audio, or on camera.

Segment 2: Values

You need to exercise:

- Fairness in portraying the crowd.
- Honesty about the difficulty of making sense of the crowd's behaviour.
- Respect for people when they collapse or become hysterical with grief.
- Responsibility in minimising the risk of harming already vulnerable people.
- Free speech in the reporting of a huge tragedy that the public must know about.

Segment 3: Principles

You know that:

- You should not portray people in an unfair light.
- You should not risk misleading your audience by providing them with information that you know will soon be out of date and which, in any case, you do not understand yourself.
- People have the right to grieve without being intruded upon.
- You should not do unnecessary harm, especially to vulnerable people.
- There is a clear public interest in knowing about the fires and their impact on people.

Segment 4: Interests

You need to balance:

- The crowd's interest in being portrayed fairly.
- The fire captain's interest in your keeping your promise to him.
- The bereaved people's interest in not having their grief intruded on.
- Your interest in informing your audience.
- Your audience's interest in receiving a fair and accurate account.
- Your interest in safeguarding or advancing your career (if you are employed).
- Your employer's (if you have one) interest in your productivity.
- Your colleagues' (if you have them) interest in your pulling your weight.

Segment 5: Loyalties

This is where you have to prioritise those interests according to the weight of loyalty that you attach to each. There are no hiding places here. You can delude yourself, but you can't hide from yourself. Here are three (of many) possible scenarios.

1. You are a highly ambitious reporter keen to make a name for yourself by breaking stories and going hard after them, zealous in pursuit of your ideal of fulfilling what you think of as 'the public's right to know'. In your personal values-system, there is no higher ideal. You have spent some time as a police-rounds reporter. You have never flinched at crime scenes, and you are always willing to do 'death knocks' — knocking on the door of bereaved people to get an interview. How will you prioritise your loyalties to those various interests?

2. You are a reporter of some experience, but your work has consisted of covering areas of social policy, and you have no previous experience of covering disasters. You haven't even attended a motor accident. For the past two years you have been reporting health, an area where you have found it most productive to take a thoughtful and cautious approach, since that seems to engender the most co-operative response from the health professionals you deal with. It also suits your temperament. But your confidence in your ability to cover this story is shaky, and you worry about letting your organisation down. How will you prioritise your loyalties here?

3. You are a very senior reporter with a reputation for excellence in covering a wide range of stories. You have been a foreign correspondent, during which you covered a major civil war. You have seen mass-grave exhumations. You have had a gun held to your head. You don't frighten easily, but you have seen a lot of human suffering, and you are conscious of the harm you can do by ill-informed reporting. You are no psychologist, but you have seen the

psychological impact that trauma has on people. How will you prioritise your loyalties here?

This exercise is based on a real-life case arising from the Black Saturday bushfires in Victoria in February 2009. The actual reporter concerned is the one described in the third scenario. His decision was to ring the newsdesk and tell them there would not be a story from him that evening. Why? He explained it this way:

First, he was troubled that if he reported the crowd in its exuberant state, he would have been at risk of unfairly portraying them as either heartless or bizarre. He himself did not understand the psychology of that crowd, had no way of obtaining such an understanding, and so could not make sense of what he had seen. He thought it would simply puzzle his readers. He also knew that by the time the story appeared the next day, that description of the mood of the crowd would have been hopelessly out of date, so any impression would probably have been misleading and unfair, without adding to the public's store of truthful information.

He had also promised the fire captain that he would respect the privacy of the people's grief. That was a promise he considered binding. Specifically, while he had witnessed the young man in his extreme grief, he decided on the grounds of human dignity and out of respect for the young man's right to the privacy of his grief — which arose, after all, from the essentially private nature of his loss — that to report his reaction would be an invasion of that privacy, with no balancing public interest.

He did not consider the fact that the grieving was done in a public place to be relevant in this case. The young man had heard of his loss publicly, so he had only grieved publicly because of those circumstances.

We can see that the reporter prioritised his loyalties this way:

1. The crowd as a whole
2. Individuals in the crowd
3. The fire captain
4. The readership of his paper
5. The public at large
6. The newspaper
7. His career

This was not an easy choice. However, it was made easier for this reporter by two factors. First, he thought — but did not know for sure — that there were no other media present, so the risk of competitive disadvantage seemed small. Second, he was a very senior reporter, highly respected by the newsroom and the newspaper's executives, and immensely experienced in covering disasters. When a reporter of this stature says he will not be sending a story, that is the end of the matter. Management doesn't second-guess him. The corollary of this is that you become a reporter of stature by having moral fibre, as well as professional talent.

We have seen how the modified Potter Box can be used as a tool for helping us to think systematically about ethical issues. It cannot make the decision for us. We must do that, and take responsibility for it. If we think thoroughly and systematically about ethical dilemmas, and do so in good faith and with intellectual integrity, we will make decisions that are ethically defensible. We will also be able to explain how we arrived at them.

There is not always a clear-cut right or wrong answer in these situations, and competent people of good will can arrive at different decisions. We can respect that, if the decisions have been arrived at by sound ethical reasoning, based on relevant values and principles.

There are other tools and frameworks, too, that can help us reason our way through ethical dilemmas. Stephen Ward proposes a four-stage model: (1) Awareness; (2) Analysis; (3) Evaluation; and (4) Judgment.[1] Stage 1 involves recognising that an ethical problem exists — a sense of discomfort, a twinge of conscience, sometimes outright recognition that an action looks questionable or that maybe you shouldn't do it. Stage 2 involves analysing the ethical issue. It is equivalent to the Values and Principles segments in the Potter Box: what are the values and principles at stake here? At Stage 3, we evaluate the options for resolving the ethical problem: perhaps it is not to pursue the story, or not to pursue it using those methods; perhaps not to publish, or at least not to publish until more checking is done. Stage 4 involves making the decision as to what is the best thing to do in all the circumstances.

Another, somewhat more complex, model was proposed by Rushworth Kidder, a journalist, who developed a nine-point checklist that broke down Ward's model and the Potter Box approach.[2] Broadly speaking, it also consisted of recognising that there was an ethical problem, putting together the relevant factual situation, identifying values and principles (which he broke down into three steps), investigating the options, and making and reflecting on a decision.

There is a common core to these three models:

- Recognise that you face an ethical problem.
- Identify the facts that have created it.
- Identify the values at stake.
- Identify the principles governed by those values.
- Identify the options for resolving the issue.
- Choose an option that is the best available.

The particular advantage of the Potter Box is that it forces us to develop reasons for choosing a particular option, based on the relevant interests at stake and the way we prioritise our loyalties. This makes us articulate our reasons to ourselves, and makes them transparent to others. In the digital age, when we can be called to account more readily and more publicly than in the past, this is a significant advantage.

CHAPTER EIGHT
CONSENT

Consent, as it applies to the practice of journalism, raises some peculiarly difficult ethical questions involving the values of honesty, fairness, and responsibility, yet it is rarely referred to in the codes. Moreover, in journalism the issue of consent has a dimension that does not generally exist for other professions: there are circumstances in which a journalist will not and should not be required to obtain it, as it would obviously be wrong to conclude that journalists ought to write only about people who have given their consent. Explicit consent is not required, for example, when politicians or others in positions of power become involved in media encounters as part of their professional lives, or when people hold press conferences or speak at public meetings, or are participants in forums such as parliament and the courts, nor when people are the object of disclosures about their criminality or wrongdoing.

In general, then, the requirement to obtain consent will vary according to the subject's familiarity with the media, position of power relative to the media's power, position as a participant in a public forum, or position as the object of disclosure of some matter that is in the public interest. For the most part, however, obtaining consent is a basic ethical requirement. Its foundational importance lies in its centrality to the exercising of personal autonomy.

Autonomy, in the liberal tradition, is generally understood as self-determination, the essence of being human.[1] It has also been characterised in libertarian terms as the freedom to pursue one's own ambitions and desires, so long as in doing so we do not infringe upon the same freedom in others — which is close to the concept of individual liberty articulated by John Stuart Mill. Mill asserted that the only purpose for which power may be rightfully exercised over another person against his will is to prevent harm to others. This is an injunction against coercion.

The philosophical arguments of Immanuel Kant complement Mill in this context. Kant adds weight to the consideration of personal autonomy with his formulation of the categorical imperative that people should never be treated as a means, but as an end only. This is an injunction against exploitation.

Injunctions against exploitation and coercion are to be found in many of the codes, but especially in those concerning respect for persons and for their interests, particularly privacy. It is in this way that a thread can be discerned connecting the codes, via the value of autonomy, to the requirement of consent, among others. However, it is left to us as individual practitioners to infer these meanings from the codes' broad abstractions.

Autonomy and capacity

An understanding of the nature and importance of consent begins with consideration of what it means to be autonomous. Related to this is the question of whether a person has the capacity or the competence to make a decision. It has been posited that competence consists of three contributory capacities: cognitive, emotional, and valuational.[2] Cognitive competence relates to a person's ability to make rational decisions. Emotional competence recognises that the decisions a person makes will be influenced by their feelings — about others as well as themselves. Valuational competence concerns the weight a person gives to the various values that might be relevant to a decision.

Assessing the capacity to consent

There has been only limited research conducted into consent capacity, and no widely accepted curricula for teaching how to assess it, even to medical practitioners.[3] As a result, it falls to the professional — in whatever field — to make this assessment. While the risks inherent in a journalistic intervention are clearly less serious than, say, a medical intervention, there is nonetheless a real risk of harm. Where there is risk of further harm to an already vulnerable person — for example, the traumatised survivor or victim of a disaster — it cannot be written off as minimal. Therefore, assessing people's capacity to consent is part of our ethical duty. A widely accepted model for assessing the capacity of people to consent is the 'four abilities' model. These are the abilities to express a choice; to understand the meaning of what is proposed; to appreciate the implications and consequences; and to arrive at a reasoned decision, once equipped with the necessary facts.[4]

Thus, it may be seen that the ability merely to express a choice is a necessary but not sufficient condition to demonstrate capacity. Ethically, the onus is on the professional practitioner to make a judgment about the extent to which the potential subject exhibits these abilities, and to respond accordingly.

Types of consent

We can learn to think more deeply about this by looking at ethical and legal developments in the field of medicine. While the *legal* requirements upon medical practitioners are quite different from those upon journalists, the fundamental *ethical* requirement is the same: in general, an intervention may not take place except with the consent of the subject. At the same time, it has been argued that the requirements of explicitness and specificity commonly required for genuinely informed consent in medicine present large and intractable difficulties.[5] It is further argued that it is time to fundamentally rethink 'informed consent' so that it becomes feasible — a new approach that would focus on the communicative transactions by which consent is sought, given, and refused. Central to these communicative transactions are intelligibility, relevance, accuracy, and honesty. Communicative transactions that would fail the test would be those that confused, baffled, misled, or manipulated the potential subject. These qualities of ethical communicative transactions are applicable equally to journalism and medicine.

Applicable, yes, but feasible? The notion of informed consent is relatively recent, having developed out of medical litigation in the United States during the latter half of the twentieth century, when the courts ruled that medical practitioners had a duty to inform the potential subject of 'any facts which are necessary to form the basis of an intelligent consent'. The types of facts covered by this included the nature of the disorder, the details of the proposed treatment, the risks and benefits involved, and any alternative, including no treatment.

The equivalent in journalism is that an intended interviewee is told beforehand what the journalist intends to write about; where, when, and in what context the story or item is likely to appear; how the subject will be portrayed, both in words and pictures; and the likely risks to and benefits for the subject from this public exposure.

Obviously, these requirements present severe practical difficulties. In journalism it is often impossible to know with any certainty how any given story will turn out: new information may alter the story out of recognition. The form and timing of publication are also commonly matters that are beyond the individual practitioner's control, unless they are writing for a platform they personally control, such as their own website. Nor can it be predicted with any certainty what the risks and benefits to the subject might be. In reality, then, the informed-consent standard couched in these terms is not feasible in journalism, except perhaps where the practitioner has full control over the use of the material.

However, consent obtained as a result of a communicative transaction that conforms to the standards of intelligibility, relevance, accuracy, and honesty may well be attainable.[6] Here, honesty becomes the key element. Did the practitioner place before the potential subject as full and truthful account as was then possible about the probable use of the material? A standard couched in these terms brings us closer to a less exacting standard — simple consent.

In a medical context, the consent required to meet this standard amounts to no more than an acceptance by the patient that a procedure should be performed on him or her. It does not require the medical practitioner to provide any details of exactly what would be done, the risks and benefits involved, or a longer-term prognosis.

The equivalent in journalism is that a subject agrees to an interview without any prior knowledge of what questions will be asked, or how the material from the interview will be used. This is a very low threshold, however. If the value of fairness, as promoted by the codes of ethics, has any meaning, more than this will be required. To achieve fairness, simple consent in the context of journalism requires three elements:

1. Conveying to the subject intelligible, relevant, accurate, and honest information in possession of the practitioner at the

time about the nature of the story and the intended use of the material.
2. Raising with the subject any foreseeable risks to the subject where the practitioner discerns risks.
3. Undertaking to inform the subject of unexpected developments in the story that might adversely affect the way the subject will be portrayed.

However, even simple consent is problematic in journalism when we are dealing with traumatised people. Evidence from research among survivors of the Black Saturday bushfires showed that their state of mind was such as to make even simple consent impossible.[7] Yet here was a large and important news story, coverage of which would have been seriously incomplete without the voices of survivors being heard. What standard of consent would have been reasonable in these circumstances? To assess this, it is instructive to reflect on the testimony of survivors and journalists after the bushfires.

Broadly speaking, the survivors stated that:
• they were in no fit state of mind to give informed or simple consent;
• they were, nonetheless, able to give or withhold consent of a kind that turned out to be sufficient for the purposes in the great majority of cases;
• many had specific reasons for wanting to speak to the media;
• in all cases but four, they subsequently stated that their decision concerning consent had been vindicated inasmuch as their reasons for speaking had been fulfilled in the media coverage, or other, unforeseen, benefits had been obtained; and
• the media encounters had done them more good than harm.

Broadly speaking, the media practitioners who covered the fires agreed that:

- prior consent of survivors was required where it was likely they would be identifiable to themselves, even if not to others;
- people should be asked once only, and a refusal should be accepted; and
- traumatised people could, and did, give or withhold consent.

How that consent was obtained was also instructive, and was a topic on which media practitioners and survivors gave very similar evidence. The characteristics of what both groups considered to be ethically correct conduct were:

- adopting a quiet approach which did not pre-suppose that the survivor would consent and which gave them an opportunity to decline;
- making an honest introduction, in which the media practitioner gave his name and said whom he worked for;
- deploying a manner that was unhurried and which conveyed to the survivor that her welfare was more important than a story;
- treating the survivor as an equal, socially and intellectually;
- using open questions, which allowed the survivor to decide what to talk about and how much to tell;
- allowing the survivor to tell the story in her own way, without probing and prompting, or putting words in her mouth;
- using a tone of voice that was even and steady, not pitying, condescending, or impatient;
- employing body language that was not aggressive or intrusive; and
- making an effort to place as much control of the encounter as possible in the hands of the survivor.

Many survivors said they were aware of *believing* they were functioning normally at the time — making decisions, taking stock, trying to think about what to do next. In retrospect, however, they came to realise how abnormally they were functioning:

> We were actually surprised that we ended up being in the paper. Even though it seems ridiculous that you are talking to a reporter, but you don't make the connection at the time. You've got three million other things in your head.
>
> I look back now and I know I was in quite severe shock. I was in a weird space. The best way I could describe it is a light-hearted hysteria. And very lucky about being safe, being found. I wasn't grounded at all.
>
> A couple of days later, I realised — I had no grasp of reality, really — that our pictures would be in every major newspaper across the country, that my niece [overseas] would see me on YouTube.[8]

It is clear from these comments that many survivors, while capable of communicating a choice, were at least to some extent deficient in their abilities to fully understand what was being proposed by the media practitioner, to appreciate the implications, and to reason their way to a decision. In these circumstances, the nature of the consent given was neither informed nor simple, but instinctual. This consent was grounded in the survivor's assessment of the media practitioner's approach. The characteristics of an acceptable approach have been enumerated above. Taken together, they may be summed up as recognising and respecting the survivor's autonomy. In the aftermath of a disaster, and in the context of dealing with media, this autonomy may be expressed as the power to decide whether to speak, to whom to speak, and what to speak about.

The evidence is that this instinctual consent was sufficient in the circumstances. This proposition rests on the fact that all but four of the 27 survivors who participated in the research said they felt vindicated: they felt that, in hindsight, their decision had been the right one, and that overall the media encounter had done them more good than harm.

A hierarchy of consent

In summary, then, there is a hierarchy of types of consent: informed, simple, and instinctual consent. In journalism, gaining informed consent is generally not feasible. In most cases, the best that can be hoped for — and indeed the required standard — is simple consent. Ethically sound simple consent can be acquired if the subject is given as much accurate and honest information as the practitioner has, if the practitioner draws the subject's attention to any discernible risks, and if the practitioner commits to advising the subject if the story were to take an unexpected turn to the subject's detriment.

In the aftermath of a disaster, however, gaining even simple consent will generally not be feasible. Subjects will possess few, if any, of the abilities needed to enter into this kind of agreement. In these circumstances, gaining instinctual consent will be practical and ethically sufficient. However, there is a special onus here on the media practitioner, which may be expressed as the need to recognise and respect the survivor's autonomy. Where this duty is observed, it is likely that instinctual consent will be given.

The level of consent thus varies with the circumstances. As a general statement, what is ethically required is *valid* consent — the validity being assessed by reference to the circumstances of the case. A requirement of this kind, supported by guidance notes, would materially improve the quality of journalistic codes. The explicit presence of consent and what it means in varying circumstances would help practitioners make sound ethical decisions on a matter that can be complex and difficult.

CHAPTER NINE
TRUTH-TELLING

The values of honesty and truth-telling, both fundamental to the codes of journalistic ethics, govern a principle that goes something like this: we only publish material that we are certain — as far as we can be — is true. To borrow from Kovach and Rosenstiel again, the truth we are dealing with is 'a complicated and contradictory phenomenon, but seen as a process over time, journalism can get at it'.[1] In this context, 'truth' has two dimensions, an evaluative and a presentational one.

The evaluative dimension itself has two sides. The first consists of surveying the available evidence, asking ourselves whether the evidence-gathering has been as complete as it can be, given what we know; whether it has been tested sufficiently; and whether it provides us with a standard of proof proportional to the seriousness of the content. This proving-up process is what we call verification.

The second side of this evaluative process involves assessing the nature of the material available to us. This means asking ourselves whether the material is propaganda, public relations, or marketing; and, if the answer is yes, asking why we would publish it and what additional material might be needed to build up a reliable version of the truth.

The presentational dimension consists of choosing words and images that convey as accurately and fairly as we can the evidence that we have evaluated as having been proved up.

Creighton Burns, one of the great editors of *The Age*, spoke about the concept of truth as it applies to journalism in his 1988 Hugo Wolfsohn Memorial Lecture:

> I wonder if thoughtful readers are not asking more than newspapers can, or are likely, to deliver. They sometimes look to us for absolute truth, for thoughtful, reflective analysis of every news event no matter how complex. That is clearly beyond the daily newspaper. We are in the business of immediate and approximate truth. Ours is an activity like tent-pegging — conducted at full gallop.[2]

This was not an apologia for sloppiness, recklessness, or haste, but a frank assertion of the realities of professional life for those engaged in journalism. If we waited for the full truth about everything — even assuming it was attainable — we would publish very little. It is a question of ethical judgment about when the material to hand has been proved up to a standard proportional to its gravity.

Burns's authority on this matter is considerable. It was he who made one of the most difficult, complex, and consequential decisions on verification in Australian journalism: the decision to publish what became known at '*The Age* Tapes'. It is a case study that has much to teach us.

Beginning some time in the late 1960s or early 1970s, the New South Wales police embarked on an elaborate operation designed to gain criminal intelligence by the use of telephone taps for which they had no legal authority. One consequence of this was that any recordings they made would be inadmissible as evidence in court.

In the early 1980s, in the course of this operation, they tapped the phone of a Sydney solicitor, Morgan Ryan, as part of a broad investigation into organised crime. One collection of conversations revealed an array of contacts that had been cultivated by Ryan, including a judge. There were conversations on the tapes between Ryan and the judge.

Some of the tapes from the operation against Ryan, as well as some transcripts from them, were obtained by a well-known crime reporter, Bob Bottom. Bottom has never revealed his source for this material, saying it was obtained in confidence. (In his later books on the subject, Bottom wrote that the materials covered 3,980 conversations.)[3]

The legal difficulties surrounding the publication of this material were considerable. One attempt was made through a Fairfax weekly newspaper, *The National Times*, but the excisions and oblique references required to make it legally safe meant that the resultant story was more or less unintelligible to the ordinary reader. There was no public reaction. However, it was now obvious to the police generally and to the state government that the tapes had been leaked, and Bottom was warned by his police contacts to get himself and the tapes out of reach of the New South Wales authorities. He thereupon went to Melbourne, and took the tapes to *The Age*.

Creighton Burns, the editor, was away, and the acting editor, Robert Haupt, set in train a process to try to authenticate the tapes. The first step was to verify that the tapes had been made by the New South Wales police in the circumstances already described. Bottom was able to provide sufficient evidence of this to persuade the newspaper that this was true. However, there were two further major questions that needed answering. Were the contents of the tapes what they appeared to be, or had they been spliced to create an incriminating context for what might have been otherwise innocent remarks? And did the voice of the person thought to be a judge belong to Lionel Murphy, a justice of the High Court of Australia, as was supposed from its distinctively gravelly tone? The tapes were submitted for analysis to a subsidiary company of *The Age* that had the equipment and expertise to detect splicing and to make voice-recognition assessments. The analysis revealed no evidence of splicing; but, on the question of voice recognition, the findings were ambiguous. Further checks on the authenticity of the tapes were carried out by the newspaper through sources inside and outside the police.

The situation confronting Burns when he returned to work was extraordinarily complex. He had material suggesting serious impropriety by one of the seven judges of Australia's highest court. The public interest in such a matter was very great, but the consequences — for the judge, the High Court, and the newspaper — were also very serious, and would be so regardless of whether the allegations of impropriety were right or wrong. The act of publication itself would have immense repercussions.

Burns made a decision to publish what he could verify — that the tapes had come from the New South Wales police, that they had not been confected, that they had been made as part of an investigation into organised crime, and that they revealed what appeared to be serious wrongdoing, including by public figures. But he would not publish what he could not verify — that the voice belonged to Justice Murphy. This meant he decided to publish as much of the content of the tapes as was necessary to reveal the nature of the material they contained, but not to identify the judge. The front-page article, headed 'Network of Influence', appeared on 2 February 1984.

What happened next demonstrated how the work of the media in making serious disclosures such as this can be taken up by other institutions — and then assume a life of its own. There was a debate in the Queensland parliament about the matter, during which Murphy was named under parliamentary privilege. This meant that the member of parliament could not be sued for his action. Moreover, fair and accurate accounts of those parliamentary proceedings could be published by the media under the protection of a form of qualified privilege called 'protected report'. It was in this way that Justice Murphy's name became linked in public to the tapes.

The following month, in March 1984, the first of two Senate select committees of inquiry into the conduct of Justice Murphy was established. The second select committee was established specifically to investigate an allegation by the then chairman of the Bench of Stipendiary Magistrates of New South Wales, Clarrie Briese, that Murphy had attempted to influence the outcome of a conspiracy case before the magistrate's court in which Morgan Ryan was the defendant. Ryan and Murphy had known each other for many years.

The report of the second committee recounted a series of conversations between Briese and Murphy concerning two matters: efforts by Briese to secure the passage of legislation through the New South Wales parliament conferring independence on magistrates, and the use by prosecuting authorities of conspiracy charges when they were finding it hard to make more substantive charges stick. In this context, Murphy had told him that the conspiracy case against Ryan was weak. Briese had agreed to look into it.

The crucial allegation by Briese was that, some days later, Murphy had rung him to say he had spoken to the New South Wales attorney-general about the independence of the magistracy, and had been told that the government intended to legislate for this. He had then said to Briese: 'Now, what about my little mate?' This was a reference to Morgan Ryan. Murphy said his recollection was that he did not use the phrase 'my little mate'.

By a three-to-one majority, the committee found that, on the balance of probabilities, Murphy had spoken and acted as he did towards Briese in an attempt to influence the outcome of the proceedings in the magistrate's court. Justice Murphy was subsequently charged with conspiring to pervert the course of justice. He was convicted, but his conviction was quashed by the New South Wales Court of Appeal. He was granted a re-trial and was acquitted. He died shortly thereafter.

In 1985, a royal commission of inquiry was established by the federal government to investigate the actions of the New South Wales police in making the tapes. The royal commission found that the tapes were indeed genuine.[4]

We can take many lessons from this case.

First, it looks a lot more cut-and-dried in a short summary like this than it was at the time. The entire process was played out over three or four years. Immense condemnation was heaped on *The Age* and on Burns personally for publishing the material. He and the newspaper were accused of having conspired to bring down a great reforming justice because he came from the left. (Lionel Murphy had been a reformist attorney-general in the Labor government of Gough Whitlam in the early 1970s, and he was a strong judicial activist on an otherwise very black-letter-law High Court.) Therefore, the first lesson is that our motives can be impugned, so we need to examine them closely ourselves beforehand. If we have acted in bad faith, it will not go well for us publicly. Even if we have acted in good faith, it might be difficult.

Second, there were indeed consequences for *The Age* and the editorial staff involved. Aside from the condemnation, they were then required to co-operate with subsequent inquiries by the Australian Federal Police and a royal commission. The newspaper had revealed itself as the possessor of information and evidence central to the commission's investigations. Having been the agent by which this had been made public, leading to the establishment of the royal commission, it could not in conscience have then declined to co-operate. And even if it had declined to help voluntarily, it would have been compelled to do so. Royal commissions have wide powers to compel the production of documents and the attendance of witnesses, and they are examined under oath, thereby bringing the laws of contempt and perjury into play. So the second lesson is that our verification procedures can be subjected to intense scrutiny; and if we are found wanting, our reputations will be damaged, and we may face big legal problems.

Third, in the light of *The Age*'s experience, we can reflect on the standard of proof that journalism can reasonably be held to. People involved in journalism — and that includes big media organisations — have no legal or formal powers of investigation. We cannot seize or demand documents. We cannot insist that people submit to an interview. We can't arrest or detain people, or obtain warrants to conduct searches of their premises. So if society expects journalism to disclose serious wrongdoing without formal powers of investigation, it is plainly unreasonable to hold people who do this kind of journalism to the same standards of proof that are needed to succeed in a court of law. On the other hand, it is equally unreasonable to accept that we can simply publish damaging material without some degree of proof that it is true.

What standard of proof is required? There are two parts to the answer. The first is that the more serious the allegation, the higher the standard of proof. At the lower end of this scale, if someone makes an accusation against someone else in a routine argument, it is usually enough to put that accusation to the other person, and obtain and publish their response. Say, for instance, that in an industrial dispute a trade-union official accuses the employer of using scab labour. It will usually be enough to put this to the employer and publish the response. There is no ethical requirement to independently investigate whether it is true before publishing. Of course, it may suggest a line of inquiry for us to pursue independently for a later story.

At the other end of the scale, let us look at the standard of proof that Creighton Burns set for himself in *The Age* Tapes case. The allegations here were of grave wrongdoing by a senior judge. It was at the top end of the scale of seriousness that anyone engaged in journalism is likely to deal with. The origin of the tapes had been verified; the fact that they had not been spliced had been verified. These facts constituted what the law calls a *prima facie* case: that is, on the face of it, someone has a case to answer here. This is the standard usually applied in committal proceedings before a magistrate. In these proceedings, a magistrate has to decide whether, on the evidence, an accused person has a case to answer before a higher court. That is all. The magistrate is not required to try the case. *The Age*, in the tapes case, could not try the matter. Its duty to society was to draw attention to evidence that showed there was a case to answer. It was then for the institutions that did have formal legal powers of investigation to take the matter up.

In between these two extremes, there are many cases where it will not be good enough to accept one person's word, or one person's word against another's. First, accepting just one person's word where any sort of negative allegation is made is dangerously thin and incomplete. Second, presenting one person's word against another usually doesn't help the audience very much. How are they to choose between them? A good ethical standard of verification involves a process of triangulation — finding some independent source of evidence in addition to the protagonists. This can often be found in publicly available documents — court records, company registers, land-title documents, annual reports of corporations or government agencies, or documents obtainable under Freedom of Information. Otherwise it might be obtained from asking an independent person with the relevant expertise to make an assessment.

For example, say a woman comes forward, claiming she has been assaulted by person X, and she points to fresh injuries on her face and neck as proof. She also says she has taken out an apprehended violence order (AVO) against person X. We believe there is a public interest in running the story if it is true, so we put these allegations to person X. He denies the assault, and says the injuries were caused in some other way or by someone else. What should we do? As it turns out, triangulating this is straightforward: we go to the court records and find out whether there is indeed an AVO, and against whom. We then go back to our protagonists with what we have found, and put it to them. This might mean that the story evaporates, of course, but that is the ethically correct outcome.

It is commonplace in newsrooms for people to ask each other: 'Do you reckon this stands up?' This is a question about verification. The person asked to make the assessment will look first at the level of corroboration. Has the person who is the subject of the story been interviewed? If not, why not? If so, was the issue put to them in the terms described in the copy, and is their response adequately reported? Where is the evidence to support any negative or harmful content? How good is that evidence? Is it good enough to justify the gravity of the allegation? Have we worded it all accurately? Have we left anything important out? Is there another possible explanation? These are the questions that vigilant editorial gatekeepers ask every day, and if we are working on our own, they are the sort of questions we need to ask ourselves.

Assessing propaganda can be especially difficult, but it is also especially important to do so. The difficulty arises because propaganda is often political in nature, and we need to know where to strike a balance between respecting freedom of political speech and supplying the oxygen of publicity to a cause. And propaganda — defined broadly as self-promoting, selective, and manipulative communications — is burgeoning. Enabled by digital technology, big corporations, government departments, and large organisations such as major sporting bodies have developed their own 'newsrooms' to supply ready-for-publication content to the media. The same technology, meanwhile, has stripped out the resources of traditional media newsrooms, making it harder for them to verify this material, and increasing the temptation for strapped news organisations to simply republish it.

In July 2013, for example, the Australian Department of Immigration and Citizenship published on its 'newsroom' website an image of what purported to be a female asylum-seeker in apparent despair at having just been told that she would be processed in Papua New Guinea and that, if she were a genuine refugee, she would be settled there and not in Australia. This image was posted just three days after the Australian prime minister, Kevin Rudd, had announced this policy as part of his election-campaign commitment to get tough with asylum-seekers who arrived by boat.

Statements by the department made it clear that this was a propaganda image designed to deter asylum-seekers from embarking on an attempt to reach Australia by boat. However, the image itself was impossible to verify independently. The department said it had been taken by one of its officers for official purposes, but no media had been allowed access to the place where it was taken, to the person who took it, or to the woman pictured, in order to verify that it was what it purported to be. Thus the media were confronted with a dual problem: was the picture genuine, and should they give oxygen to an obvious piece of propaganda, even though the issue of asylum-seekers was a matter of clear public interest?

The issue was further complicated by the fact that, in the overheated atmosphere of the 2013 federal election campaign, in which the treatment of asylum-seekers was a major issue, the image also had naked political propaganda value.

In the end, the media that published the picture did so while issuing a caveat that it had not been verified.

These judgments are hard enough to make when the propaganda takes a form that does not violate the law or advance a cause which is harmful to the community's interests. However, propaganda that does cause harm requires us to strike the balance differently. In these cases, the balance is between promoting freedom of speech and minimising harm. It is a much more severe test, since to supply oxygen to this kind of propaganda is to become party to increasing the risk of harm.

For example, in London in 2013, a soldier was killed in a busy street outside his barracks by two men who claimed to be Islamists exacting revenge for what the British military were doing in the Afghanistan war. The killing itself was clearly news and a matter of great public interest. So was the self-proclaimed motive, declared by one of the killers. With bloodied hands, he stood on the footpath a few metres away from the dying man and delivered to camera a lengthy apologia for the crime. The ethical question for those making journalistic judgments about this was: how much of this apologia was it necessary to transmit in order for the audience to gain an understanding of the killers' motive and make some assessment of the killers themselves? Once that minimal purpose had been achieved, the ethical justification for continuing to broadcast the apologia evaporated. Otherwise, the coverage would have become a platform for propaganda.

Assessing public relations or marketing material is much more routine; it is a daily challenge. We fail our duty to the ethic of truth-telling if we simply recycle or re-package as 'news' these kinds of untested or uncontested material. This challenge has become harder to deal with as the resources available for journalism — especially in the large newspaper companies — have shrunk as a result of the impact of the Internet on their advertising revenues.

The digital revolution has also added a new layer of complexity to journalistic verification. First, it has added exponentially to the sheer volume of information available to us. (The vast tranche of data released by WikiLeaks is an example of this.) Second, it has made available to us enormous bodies of data that would have been neither available nor manageable in the past. This gives us the opportunity to give our audiences access to information on an unprecedented scale, so that they may see a much fuller version of the evidence on which our stories are based, and come to their own conclusions.

However, quantity is no guarantee of quality. As Nate Silver wrote in his penetrating and insightful study of probability and prediction, because the volume of information is increasing exponentially, and relatively little of it is useful, we need to develop better ways to distinguish the signal from the noise.[5]

In a general sense, this imposes a more demanding standard of verification on us as journalists, since it is us whom the community increasingly relies on to make this distinction — sifting information, misinformation, and disinformation. And this confronts us with the necessity to challenge two ingrained elements of the journalistic culture. One is the triumph of drama over probability: the habit of our professional mind to write about the most dramatic possibility — no matter how remote — rather than the likeliest probability. The second is our propensity to present as certainties things that are only approximations or estimates.

An everyday example is the way we tend to present the results of public-opinion polls. Polls are based on samples of the relevant population — say, people eligible to vote — and all samples, no matter how carefully drawn and weighted, carry the risk of statistical error. Most opinion polls commissioned by the Australian media are based on random samples of 1,000 people or so, and statisticians know that a sample of this size and type will yield a sampling error of plus or minus about 3 per cent at the 95 per cent confidence level (meaning that, 95 times out of 100, the results will fall within that margin of error). So a movement of up to three percentage points in either direction from one poll to another lies within the margin of error, and cannot be said to indicate change. Yet it is common to see such movements reported as if they did so. This is a case where we have verified and verifiable data, and yet we choose to represent it in a way that is misleading. It is an ethical failure, a failure of truth-telling.

It is symptomatic of a wider problem in journalism — the craving for certainty. It is doubtless related to the news value of clarity (see chapter five): we want the story to be as simple and conclusive as possible. Uncertainty is the enemy here. Yet the world is full of uncertainties, and to present as certainties matters that contain uncertainties is a failure of truth-telling. Conversely, where there is an absence of certainty, we are inclined to disbelieve it: either it is a certainty, or it is not to be believed at all. This is a weakness in media practice that has long been exploited by politicians and public-relations people.

Among the most damaging examples of the way this works to the detriment of the public interest is the way the tobacco industry ran a successful media strategy for decades based on the argument that there was no absolutely conclusive scientific evidence to show a causal connection between smoking and lung cancer. In reality, conclusive evidence of causality is not easy to establish, either in the natural or the social sciences, but that does not leave us with only theoretical speculations to work from. Between these two extremes there often lies a large field of strong hypotheses, where the weight of evidence clearly points in one direction. And smoking was such a case: there was a strong hypothesis, with plenty of evidence to support it, that smoking did indeed cause lung cancer, but the tobacco industry was able to play the media off a break by insisting that the connection was not proven.

Much the same is happening nowadays in the debate about climate change. There is a high consensus among scientists in the relevant fields that anthropogenic climate change is real and is a cause of global warming. There is much less consensus about the rate of warming and its likely consequences, but that does not derogate from the existence of the consensus about the core issue. Those who wish to argue against the case for global warming have exploited the lack of consensus about the consequences, and have been successful in harnessing some elements of the media by concentrating on this uncertainty.

A commitment to the ethical requirement of truth-telling requires us to pay careful attention to these evidentiary considerations, to make diligent inquiries until we ourselves are able to make a well-informed lay assessment about the evidence, and to report on the issue accordingly. We need to wean ourselves off certainty.

There is one more aspect to this question of verification, and it, too, has emerged with the advent of the Internet. Ethically, verification must take place prior to publication, not afterwards. The so-called 24/7 news cycle has put this requirement under great pressure. It has led us to think that our primary duty is to be first. There is even a face-saving mantra, 'If it's wrong, it won't be wrong for long.' In other words, someone will see the error and draw it to our attention, and the technology will enable us to correct it quickly. This is ethically indefensible. Our primary duty is to be right. Society gains nothing and loses something from misinformation, and once we have published any story, we can't get it back. Someone will have seen it, and all our later efforts to correct it will be insufficient. As Omar Khayyam wrote in the *Rubaiyat* nine hundred years ago:

> The moving finger writes; and, having writ
> Moves on: nor all thy piety nor wit
> Shall lure it back to cancel half a line,
> Nor all thy tears wash out a word of it.

CHAPTER TEN
SOURCES AND CONFIDENCES

The problems raised by the need for confidentiality and source protection are some of the most difficult ethical issues faced by those engaged in journalism. An obligation of confidentiality can arise in either of two ways. The person giving us material may say explicitly that he or she is supplying it in confidence — in which case, if we accept it, we have automatically agreed to keep it confidential. Or we might receive information or other material in circumstances where it is obvious to a reasonable person that it is being given in confidence. For example, if someone in the course of an interview begins to drift into details of a recent medical procedure that has nothing to do with the subject matter of the interview, it would be obvious to a reasonable person that this part of the conversation is being conducted in confidence. We hear him out, but we don't use that material, because we recognise it as having been given in confidence.

The ethical difficulties begin when someone wants to give us material in confidence, or when we go to someone seeking information, and they say they will only give it in confidence. When this happens — as it does fairly frequently — we need to know what we are getting into.

Often, we are not getting into anything very deep, because the source just wants to give us some gossip that does not amount to a story or even a hint of a story. We treat the material in confidence, of course, but there are not likely to be any consequences because there is not likely to be anything published. But when the material amounts to something of substance, and a real story might ensue, we need to carefully consider what obligations and consequences can follow.

The rules and conventions

In a journalistic setting, the starting point is to know the status of any material imparted to us professionally. That applies in all cases. It is essential to be sure about whether the material is being given on the record, on background, or off the record. There is a lot of confusion about this among journalists and their sources, because the latter two terms are often used interchangeably. However, there is now a broad consensus in the professional literature about what these terms mean.

'On the record' means that any material from the source may be published, and the source identified. 'On background' means that material from the source may be published, but not in a way that attributes it to or identifies the source. 'Off the record' means that the material may not be published at all, and the interaction between the journalist and the source is itself confidential.

We may use the latter information as a lead or cue to pursue a story, but in doing so we must not give away the source. It becomes our responsibility to verify the material, but in doing so we must take all reasonable steps to protect the identity of our source — being sparing about copying any material, securing the originals, and securing any other material than might tend to identify him or her. We also need to be very cautious about writing down anything that will identify the source, even in our own computers. The legal processes of discovery and subpoena can reach into our computers, our homes, our filing cabinets, and our notebooks.

It is of the first importance in dealing with sources that both parties are clear about the status of the information-exchange prospectively — that is, before any information is provided — not retrospectively. People who are used to dealing with the media will know without being told that if they are talking to a reporter with a recorder on or notes being taken, then they are on the record. But people who are not familiar with media practice may not know this. They might — and commonly do — think that they are just chatting, and that if we want to use any of it, we will ask them. So when we are dealing with people like this, we need to be upfront right from the start: we need to explain that we would like to make a note or a recording of what they are saying, because we may want to use it in a story.

Sometimes, however, people who are unfamiliar with the media get into deep water before they realise it, and, when the realisation dawns, become panic-stricken. An example of this occurred in Sydney when a young reporter on a suburban newspaper got an unsolicited phone call from a senior nurse at the local hospital. She told him that the paper needed to investigate the lack of security for emergency-department staff, because people under the influence of drugs were assaulting the staff and causing a lot of injuries. Management had been told, but had done nothing.

All this was out of her mouth before she realised that the reporter would want to quote her as having said it. Her intention had been just to tip him off. She then back-tracked, and begged the reporter to treat what she had said in confidence, saying she would lose her job if it became known to the hospital that she had disclosed this information. The reporter, realising that here was a person who had no media experience at all, did the ethically correct thing and agreed retrospectively to treat the material as off the record. He was able to confirm the details through the nurses' union, the local health authority, and the police, and got his story that way. In this case, a retrospective agreement to treat information as off the record was ethically justified because of the informant's ignorance of media practice.

Negotiating off-the-record arrangements

In journalism, we are generally in the business of getting hold of material that we can publish. That is what we do. That is what society expects of us. So going off the record is not to be done without good reason, and it needs to be done with care. As it happens, there are circumstances in which the public interest is served by disclosure of information that is not attributed to its source — such as the disclosure of corruption, or malpractice, or serious harm. In making a decision about whether to accept information off the record, factors to consider are:

- The seriousness of the subject-matter.
- The informant's motives.
- The possible consequences for the informant if he or she is identified.
- The consequences for us, as individuals and any organisation we might be working for, of keeping the secret.

On seriousness, the material might be assessed using a public-interest test of the kind discussed in chapter four, which might be briefly stated in these terms: 'The public interest concerns matters that affect the citizens' capacity to participate in civic life; public health, safety, or financial security; or the conduct of affairs in which the public have invested trust.'

It is also important to establish whether the information is first-hand, or hearsay, or merely gossip. It needs to be first-hand to justify receiving it off the record. We can get hearsay or gossip anywhere, and, in any case, it goes to the issue of motive. A person who asks us to trade in hearsay or gossip is likely to have a questionable motive for doing so, because these are questionable categories of information. It is important to explore and assess this.

Sometimes informants will be driven by frustration combined with good-faith determination, because the matter is clearly in the public interest and they have tried unsuccessfully to have it ventilated and fixed internally. This is the classic position of the whistleblower. Sometimes, however, people want to use anonymity as a cloak from under which they can make unsubstantiated or malicious allegations, or harm a rival, or achieve an ambition for themselves at someone else's expense. And sometimes they have become obsessed by some real or perceived injustice, and cannot rest until it is out in the open, hoping that this will bring them either revenge or vindication. It can be quite hard to deal with this third group, because while it is not uncommon to find that they have become irrational, there is also usually a kernel of truth in their allegations, or at least there is some right on their side.

We need to know what the motive is. If we agree to receive material off the record without knowing why, we run the risk of becoming a cat's paw for the informant. This is scandalous behaviour for a journalist to engage in, apart from being naïve and incompetent. It is not enough that anonymity merely serves the source's convenience or ours. The information that the source is conveying should serve the public interest.

Assessing the risk to the source is a very important consideration. People who disclose wrongdoing, or embarrass or harm powerful interests such as governments and big corporations, often take big risks in doing so. They might lose their jobs, and might find it hard to get another one. In this way, they jeopardise their own and their family's economic security. Or they might be shunned by their colleagues, and their career prospects might be ruined, even if they are not sacked. They might be at risk of retaliation, including violent retaliation. These are strong reasons to want anonymity, and equally strong reasons why promises of confidentiality, once given, must be maintained.

The source may be well aware of the possible consequences of his or her identity's coming out, but sometimes people are blinded by zeal, and we need to be sure that they have thought carefully about any risks they might run by making their disclosures. These may include risks they previously hadn't thought of, because they hadn't understood the consequences for us. Once they have confided in us and we have published the material, their fate, in respect of any risks involved, will be to a considerable extent in our hands.

The biggest risk to us — and consequently to the source — is that the story might provoke a court case, or a commission of inquiry, where we are called to give evidence. Even without our disclosing the source's identity, he or she might be identified as a result of investigations into the matters raised by our story. This occurred in a case in 2007 involving two reporters on the *Herald Sun* newspaper in Melbourne who published a story based on off-the-record material about the administration of certain benefits to ex-servicemen by the Department of Veterans' Affairs.

The journalists refused to reveal the identity of their source, and were each fined $7,000 for contempt in the Victorian County Court, despite the fact that the source was identified anyway by members of the Australian Federal Police investigating the leak.[1] The identification was achieved by using a combination of closed-circuit television footage and telephone records. The footage showed the informant on the telephone, and the telephone records showed that he had talked to the reporters.

The most extreme recent case of adverse consequences for an informant concerned Dr David Kelly, a national-security specialist in Britain. He was revealed as the source for a BBC report that the intelligence on which the 2003 invasion of Iraq was based had been 'sexed up', or interpreted in an exaggerated way to justify the invasion. Dr Kelly was aggressively questioned before a committee of the British parliament about his role as the BBC's source, and was found dead two days later. A judicial inquiry found that he had committed suicide; however, there was no inquest, and the cause of his death remained a matter of controversy in Britain for more than a decade, with allegations that government security services murdered him.

It is because of the potential for severe harm to confidential informants that most codes of ethics impose an absolute obligation on us to protect the identity of an off-the-record source. A secondary but nonetheless important reason is that confidential information might dry up if informants cannot trust us to keep secrets and promises. If this happened, many instances of wrongdoing would probably never come to light.

The risks to the source can be minimised or eliminated if there is some way we can get the material on the record. The source may have some ideas about this. For example, he or she might know about the existence of a file, with a file number, which could be obtained under Freedom of Information, or they might know of court proceedings where some of the material came to light and contained clues about where we could find more. Or he or she might suggest we talk to a particular person and ask a particular set of questions. Of course, in following up any ideas such as these, we must not even hint at the source's identity.

Sometimes we are tempted or pressured into attempting to disguise our sources. However, this presents us with a different ethical problem: dishonesty. We must not knowingly mislead the public to throw people off the scent of the real source — by referring, for example, to 'a parliamentary source' when actually the source works in a department of executive government. Dishonesty such as this can undermine the story as a whole and may affect our credibility as a witness in any subsequent proceedings. Above all, it breaches the trust of the public in what we write.

If we do make a promise of confidentiality, it is binding on us and, if we work for an organisation, it binds the organisation, too. Therefore, if as employees we intend to enter into an arrangement such as this, we must inform our editor. He or she may want to know at least some details about the informant so as to assess their credibility. We are obliged to give what information we are asked for (and we should have made this possibility clear to our informant at the outset). The editor's right to know derives from the fact that he or she, too, is bound by any undertakings we have made. The editor is also obliged to assess the legal exposure and the risks to the organisation's reputation, and to weigh these against any potential benefits.

The legal protections available to us if we refuse to divulge the identity of a confidential source to a court or a royal commission are limited and uncertain. So this remains, above all, an ethical question.

However, the Commonwealth, New South Wales, Victoria, and Western Australia introduced amendments to their Evidence Acts in 2011–2012, which contain what is described in the legislation as a legal privilege for journalists, exempting them from the obligation to disclose in court the identity of people from whom they receive information in confidence in the course of their professional work. These amendments are known as 'shield' laws, since they are designed to allow the identity of sources to be shielded from disclosure.

There is uncertainty and inconsistency over who is entitled to claim this privilege. The Commonwealth Act is broad, and applies to anyone involved in gathering and disseminating information to the public. This might include bloggers, citizen-journalists, or other individuals engaged in journalism. The states' amendments are narrower, however, and apply only to people 'employed' as journalists. How the courts will interpret the term 'employed' had not been tested at the time of writing. Would it include freelancers and contributors, for example?

Moreover, it is not an absolute privilege. Courts and royal commissions still have the power to require disclosure of the source's identity, but in doing so they must weigh the consequences against the benefit to the system of justice. So it is more in the nature of a discretion than a privilege. This view was affirmed by a recent judgment of the Western Australian Supreme Court in the first substantive test of the shield laws.[2] The case arose from an attempt by a mining company, Hancock Prospecting Pty Ltd, to subpoena Western Australian Newspapers and one of its journalists, Steve Pennells, for production of documents relating to articles that Pennells had written about a dispute between members of the Hancock family, in particular Gina Rinehart and some of her children. This dispute was the subject of arbitration in another court.

Pennells and the newspaper successfully claimed the privilege afforded by the WA shield laws. In the key paragraphs of her reasons for judgment, Justice Janine Pritchard gave greater weight to the public interest in the communication of facts and opinion to the public by the news media than to the public interest in the administration of justice. She gave three reasons for this. First, the probative value of the information sought under the subpoena was no more than supplementary to the evidence already before court of arbitration. In other words, the interest in the administration of justice could already be met by the existing evidence. Second, the arbitration involved a civil, not a criminal, matter, and so the liberty of a person was not at stake. Third, while there was no evidence that any harm would befall the reporter's confidential source, there was evidence that disclosure of the source would redound upon the reporter, Steve Pennells, because it would require him to breach a fundamental ethical obligation on him as a journalist to protect confidential sources from being disclosed.

On this basis — and for other reasons not germane here — Justice Pritchard held that to require the production of documents as sought under the subpoena would be oppressive and an abuse of process. The critical issues on which her judgment turned were:

- How necessary is the information in seeing justice done?
- Is anyone's liberty at stake?
- What harm risks being done either to the source or the journalist?

Justice Pritchard also made a point of saying that her findings were made in respect of the facts of this particular case only, and that her judgment did not mean that that a subpoena for the production of documents by a journalist would always fail. What is important, however, is that it has demonstrated how at least one Supreme Court justice has construed certain important aspects of the shield laws, and in particular how the competing public interests were balanced.

The states also have laws to protect whistleblowers — people in government who divulge serious wrongdoing in the public interest — but they are weak and limited, and do not confer any legal privilege on journalists. They also generally apply only to people in the public sector, except in South Australia, where they apply also to people in the private sector.

So if our confidential informant is blowing the whistle on private-sector wrongdoing, there is no protection, except in South Australia. The Commonwealth has some limited protection for private-sector whistleblowers under the Corporations Act, but relying on it without having good legal advice would be risky. In 2013, the Commonwealth also introduced a bill to protect whistleblowers in the Commonwealth public service, but it had many deficiencies and did not pass into law before the parliament rose for 2013 elections.

There is one further, but much narrower, legal avenue available to journalists for protecting their sources. It is called the Newspaper Rule. This is a rule of practice that 'guides the exercising of judicial discretion' in defamation and related actions.[3] The rule states that a journalist will not be required to divulge the identity of a source unless the court decides that it is necessary to do so in the interests of the administration of justice. So if the court decides that the case can be resolved without a journalist revealing his or her source, the journalist is excused. But if the court decides that the case cannot be resolved without the journalist identifying the source, the journalist is required to do so under pain of contempt.

Chequebook journalism

Occasionally, a relationship with a source will rest on a commercial footing, where either the journalist or the media company has offered money, or the source has demanded it, in exchange for access or information. These situations always raise serious ethical questions. At their worst, such offers by journalists or media companies are simply bribes. Between July 2011 and mid-2013, a series of allegations were made about payments by the now-defunct *News of the World* newspaper in London to officers in the London Metropolitan Police and other government agencies for access to information about people whom the newspaper wished to pursue. These became the subject of criminal prosecutions.

Even at their best, these practices are highly questionable. The obvious questions for the ethical journalist to ask are: Why would this person want money for the information? To what extent is this person likely to embellish or exaggerate the information in order to give value for money? Should I reveal to my audience that I have paid for the information? If so, how much detail do I need to provide in order to meet the requirements of transparency?

Some media organisations ban this practice outright. Others leave themselves open to the possibility of paying for information when they believe it is in the public interest or in the commercial interests of the media organisation to obtain the material. An example is given in this book in chapter twelve, when a television channel paid a person for the medical records of two Australian Football League players — records that the informant claimed to have found in the street. In 1975, *The Age* newspaper paid an informant for documents providing evidence of illegal loan-raising efforts by the then federal minister for minerals and energy, Rex Connor. The 'loans affair', as it became known, led ultimately to the political crisis in which the government of Gough Whitlam was dismissed by the governor-general, Sir John Kerr.[4]

A further objection to chequebook journalism is that it can provide a means by which criminals profit from their criminality. For example, in 1989, Channel 7 in Sydney paid a Rugby League player, Paul Hayward, $12,000 for an exclusive account of his 11 years in a Thai prison for drug-trafficking.[5]

And the purchasing of 'exclusivity', which is part and parcel of chequebook journalism, has other consequences. One is that the audiences of media outlets other than the one that paid for the story are denied access to information that in some cases is of general public interest — sometimes in circumstances where the public have paid for services, such as search and rescue. This is commonly the case after disasters from which there have been few survivors, such as the Thredbo landslide in 1997, when publicity agents will insert themselves between the media and the survivors. This can be of great practical benefit to the survivors, since it shields them from a media onslaught at a time of severe vulnerability, but it also comes at some cost to the availability of information in which the public has an interest.

Chequebook-journalism arrangements also can involve transfer of final editorial control of the story from the media outlet to the informant or the informant's agent, meaning a loss of editorial independence. Harry M. Miller, an agent who specialised in this line of work, wrote in his memoirs: 'One of the things that irritate the media when dealing with me is my insistence on full editorial control.'[6]

The issues raised by chequebook journalism, then, are motive, credibility, verification, transparency, public interest, lawfulness, integrity, and editorial independence. These are good grounds for avoiding it.

CHAPTER ELEVEN
DECEPTION AND BETRAYAL

An American academic, Tom Luljak, has written about what he calls 'the routine nature of journalistic deception'.[1] This is a shocking phrase. It implies that deception is so much a part of the practice of journalism that it happens more or less all the time, and that people engaged in journalism consider it unremarkable. He went on to say, 'Journalists tend not to see the behaviour as questionable.' This is a sweeping statement, but Luljak provides considerable evidence in the form of observational studies to support it — so much so that, in any serious discussion of journalism ethics, we cannot simply wish it away.

Luljak defines deception by using Sissela Bok's formulation. Bok is one of the foremost moral philosophers of the twentieth century, and she defines deception as occurring when:

> We communicate messages meant to mislead [others], meant to make them believe what we ourselves do not believe. We can do so through gesture, through disguise, by means of action or inaction, even through silence.[2]

Luljak spent two days in the newsroom of a regional television station in the United States, observing the journalists at work and asking them how they went about it. The station, he says, had a reputation for producing a quality news service, and had won several awards for journalistic excellence. In other words, it wasn't a cowboy outfit. What follows is a summary of cases he observed. The first two involved the station's police reporter.

In the first case, the reporter agreed to broadcast misleading information from the police, intended to make three murder suspects whom the police were investigating think the police knew more than they really did. The reporter justified his agreement by saying, 'It's a great story. They get the guys and I get the story.' He also said that he personally believed the suspects were guilty. And finally he acknowledged that it was part of the close relationship he had with the police: 'I'm pretty tight with some of them. There's a bond of mutual respect'. In the event, the broadcast did not go ahead, but that did not alter the fact that the journalist had agreed in principle to do it. This is a good illustration of the concept of journalistic capture, referred to in chapter five, when the importance of the relationship with contacts is elevated to a level that results in insufficient weight being given to other considerations, such as truth-telling.

Had he gone through with his plan, it would have involved deceiving his employers and the public at large, as well as the three murder suspects. His justification was built on three propositions:

1. He would get a good story.
2. He would be serving the public interest by helping the police to catch three murderers. (This argument rested on his belief that the three suspects were probably guilty. We do not know the basis for this belief.)
3. In helping the police like this, he was doing his part in maintaining an arrangement by which he got more

information from the police, no doubt for what he considered a combination of career-advancing and public-interest purposes.

The same reporter also had developed a bantering relationship with what was described as a 'stern-looking female clerk' in the sheriff's office, in which he 'talked dirty' to her to 'loosen her up' to get help with such things as mug shots and computer printouts on criminals. Thus he sought to develop an emotional bond as a means of getting information. He did so by encouraging her to think of him as someone who found her attractive enough to flirt with, so she would confide in him the information he wanted. It should be said that, from the examples Luljak gave, the talk could be defined as 'dirty' only in the most puritanical American sense of the word, amounting to no more than a mildly lewd pun.

In Luljak's third case, a young reporter still studying journalism at the local university was planted *incognito* in a section of the university's football ground from which the media had been explicitly banned, ostensibly for reasons concerning public safety, although Luljak's account did not nail that down very well. She was selected for the assignment because she had never appeared on camera and so was not known by sight to the general public. She asserted she had a legal right to be in the banned area, and once in there she identified herself to students she was interviewing as being from the television station. The news director who assigned her to the job did so, he said, on the basis of the 'public's right to know' what was happening in the student section of the ground where there had been an incident the previous week in which a student had had to be resuscitated.

The fourth case involved a reporter who did 'soft' interviews with people because they had either an unusual hobby, an unusual job, or something that was personally interesting — what we call 'human interest' stories. Speaking of his and his cameraman's technique, he said, 'We roll on everything', with the objective of capturing subjects in unguarded moments. He justified this by saying that people treated this way knew they were to be the subject of a television story, so he didn't 'feel bad' about recording their actions and comments, even when the subject thought that the recording equipment and camera had been turned off.

As these four examples show, not all acts of deception are alike in their seriousness, but that should not blind us to the fact that they are, in the end, examples of journalism practised in bad faith. At one end of the continuum is the behaviour illustrated by the second of Tom Luljak's examples — the police reporter's banter with the stern-looking woman in the sheriff's office. Now, uttering a mildly lewd pun might not be what a person of refined sensibilities would do, but at its most innocent this sort of exchange is no more than social ingratiation. We want some information from someone, so we pretend that he or she is the most important person in our lives at that particular moment, and that what has happened to them or what they are about to tell us is of supreme importance. If this means taking an artificially intense interest in a conversation with someone, or kidding around trying to locate their sense of humour, so be it. Much journalism — and much academic research, for that matter — would be impossible without such sleights of hand.

At the next level of the deception scale, however, we are already trespassing on the dishonest. In Luljak's third example, a reporter is assigned to gain access to a place from which the media have been banned, by disguising that fact that she is a journalist. She does her best to rectify this by declaring her true status when dealing with individual students, but any justification for this kind of deception requires a balance to be struck between the dishonesty of the conduct and the public interest to be served. It is far from clear in this case whether there was any public-interest justification. Perhaps there was a genuine issue about public safety in that part of the stadium. However, the only evidence that this might be so was that on a previous occasion a student had had to be resuscitated. For all we know, he might have had a heart attack.

The reporter in Luljak's fourth example takes a further step along the continuum, into the territory of deliberate exploitation, when he takes advantage of people's lack of media awareness to have the camera rolling as he arrives, with the intention of catching them unawares.

It is clear from these examples that there are degrees of deception. The more we seek to have people believe what we ourselves do not, the more serious the deception becomes. At the extreme end of this continuum lies entrapment. There is a law against this, but let us stick to the ethical considerations here. During the Victorian state election campaign in November 2010, a reporter on the *Herald Sun* newspaper telephoned and emailed Labor, Liberal, and Greens candidates, pretending to be an ordinary citizen concerned about law-and-order issues, and also pretending to be a member of the public wishing to make 'a substantial donation' to each of the three political parties. When a Greens staffer rang back the mobile-phone number in one of the emails, the reporter owned up to being the author of the email, and reportedly said, 'Ha, ha, ha. You've passed the test.' The purpose of the exercise evidently was to test the parties' responses to campaign-donation offers and to the issue of crime and punishment. It appears he was trying to entrap them into breaking their parties' rules on the receipt of campaign donations, or into disavowing their parties' policies on crime and punishment, or both.

At about the same time, a much larger entrapment operation, or 'sting', involving Pakistani cricketers, was mounted by *The News of the World* in London in 2010. Its investigations editor and a man called Mazher Mahmood, who was later dubbed the 'fake sheik' because of his role in this and other stings, entrapped a number of Pakistani cricketers in a betting scandal by setting up arrangements under which the players would be paid substantial sums of money to bowl no-balls at specified moments in an international match. The no-balls were duly bowled, and the newspaper then exposed the players and the sting.

As with many of the ethical dilemmas that confront us in journalism, the rights and wrongs rest on a balance between public and private interests. These two examples help us analyse how we might think about striking this balance. There are five questions to be answered in doing so.

1. Do we have reasonable grounds for suspecting wrongdoing of the kind we hope to expose?

It is quite untenable to embark on entrapment merely on speculation — on a baseless assumption that someone, somewhere, might do some wrong. If it were otherwise, none of us would be safe from attempts to entrap us every day, and the trust on which we all depend for our day-to-day dealings with others would be undermined. So we must have a reasonable basis for suspecting the wrongdoing that we are intending to expose.

2. Do we have reasonable grounds for suspecting that it is the targets of our 'sting' who are responsible, or mainly responsible, for this wrongdoing?

This is not only an ethical consideration, but a practical one. We can't mount sting operations all over the place and all the time. We must have some rational basis for believing that the targets are reasonably suspected of the wrongdoing in question.

3. Do we have some other way of getting this information? Has there been a police investigation, or an investigation by some other responsible body — say, the International Cricket Council, in the case of the Pakistani cricketers. Can we get the information from them?

4. If there is a formal investigation under way, are we likely to impede it or cause due process to miscarry?

It is easy for us to stumble into an area that is already the subject of an investigation, say by the police, and for our appearance on the scene to have the effect of tipping off the suspects, even if that was never our intention. Or if an investigation has already resulted in charges being laid, perhaps resulting in an appearance in court of which we were unaware, we may commit contempt of court by prejudicing a trial. By being diligent in trying to find out if there is some other way of getting the information, we minimise such risks.

5. Is this a matter of public interest, or merely of public curiosity?

Apply the public-interest test. Does it concern matters that affect the capacity of citizens to participate in civic life; public health, safety, or financial security; or the conduct of affairs in which the public have invested trust?

The London operation, on these criteria, was defensible. There was widespread suspicion that international cricket matches had been fixed by the bribing of players to enable people to win bets on the games. There were many grounds for suspecting that players from Pakistan were often involved in this bribery and fixing. Neither the ICC nor the police had been able to get to the bottom of it, and it was clearly a matter of public interest, since public trust in the integrity of international cricket is a big factor in people's decisions about whether to spend money attending matches, or whether to attach any importance to the results of a game in which many thousands of people have invested a lot of themselves, building their careers and reputations.

The Melbourne operation was not defensible on any criterion. There was no reasonable suspicion of wrongdoing, and so naturally there was no reasonable basis for thinking the people approached had been engaged in wrongdoing. It was entirely speculative and mischievous. There was nothing to investigate, so there was no prospect of obtaining the information any other way, and there was no public interest because nothing had happened. It was a disgraceful stunt with not one redeeming feature.

An entirely different aspect of the deception issue arises when journalists try to get access to places where they have been blocked from going. The planting of the young television reporter in the university football stadium is an example of this, but a more complex and interesting set of questions arose in the aftermath of the Black Saturday bushfires in Victoria in February 2009.

The fireground had been blocked off by police and emergency services, first because of safety considerations and then by order of the coroner, at places where people were believed to have died. This was to preserve the integrity of the scene, so that untainted scientific evidence could be gathered for forensic purposes. Journalists' reactions to being excluding demonstrated vividly the absence of an ethical consensus on this kind of predicament. Some respected the roadblocks as a legitimate as well as legal means of cordoning off the disaster area, both in order to protect any evidence from contamination and to prevent people going in, getting injured, and having to be rescued. Others, who had undergone training provided by the fire brigade, had been equipped with yellow high-visibility jackets just like those worn by firefighters. They were often waved through the roadblocks by the police, who mistook them for firefighters, and they did not stop to identify themselves as journalists. Some journalists abandoned their vehicles on the road and, away from the police, set out across the burned-out terrain on foot. Some who got into the fireground by these means then concealed their identity from the police by hiding their equipment and pretending to be residents.

Some who had befriended survivors at the relief centres were offered the chance to masquerade as family members and so qualify for a plastic wristband that police were using to identify residents. (People with wristbands were being allowed into the fireground.) Some journalists actively tried to obtain one of these bands; others were offered a wristband, but declined on ethical grounds to take them.

Accepting that there was a clear public interest in the bushfire story, what justifications, if any, might support deceptive conduct in these circumstances? The fires themselves, and the fate of the towns engulfed by them, had already been widely reported. Information was being provided by the police and other authorities about the devastation, and survivors were available to the media at relief centres outside the fire ground. There was no evidence that any factual information about what had happened was being covered up. This was obviously a situation in which factors other than the public interest were involved in the journalists' decision-making: the desire to see for themselves rather than rely on second-hand accounts; the competitive urge to find a story no one else had; and reluctance to rely only on official accounts. Against those factors had to be balanced the risks to their own safety and that of others who might have had to rescue them, had they got into trouble; the risk of contaminating what was at that time declared to be a crime scene; and the deception inherent in the ways they obtained access. It can be seen from the disparate responses that individual journalists struck this balance in very different places.

Betrayal

In 1990, an American journalist and author, Janet Malcolm, wrote a book called *The Journalist and the Murderer*, based on a two-part article on journalistic betrayal that she had written the previous year for *The New Yorker*.[3] It has since become a standard, if highly controversial, work of reference on the topic. Her thesis is uncompromising, and is summed up in her famous first two sentences:

> Every journalist who is not too stupid or too full of himself to notice what is going on knows that what he does is morally indefensible. He is a kind of confidence man, preying on people's vanity, ignorance, or loneliness, gaining their trust and betraying them without remorse.

Her argument was based on the case of Joe McGinniss and Jeffrey MacDonald. McGinniss was an author, and MacDonald, a medical practitioner, had been convicted of the murder of his pregnant wife and their two small daughters.

Prior to MacDonald's trial, McGinniss conducted an interview with him, at the end of which MacDonald asked McGinniss if he would write a book about the case from the perspective of the defence team. MacDonald needed money to help pay his legal costs, and had been sounding out other authors, too, about a book deal in which MacDonald would take a share of the proceeds. McGinniss agreed to such a deal, on the basis that he would get total access to MacDonald and his lawyers. In fact, he was made a member of the defence team so he could be privy to all discussions between MacDonald and the lawyers, including those covered by lawyer–client privilege.

In the course of the trial, at which MacDonald was convicted, McGinniss came to believe he was guilty. Nonetheless, over four years of subsequent correspondence, he led MacDonald to believe that he thought him innocent and that the book would address itself to the righting of the injustice done to him. In fact, the book, when it came out, accused MacDonald of having committed the murders, and described him as a publicity-seeker, womaniser, and latent homosexual.

Although this was obviously an extreme and unusual case, Janet Malcolm used it as the basis for her argument that all journalism is predicated on betrayal. However, it is not necessary to accept Malcolm's thesis as a whole in order to appreciate that there is a degree of truth in it. There is always the *opportunity* for those engaged in journalism to betray their subjects, but it does not follow that this betrayal always occurs, or that if it does, it occurs on such a harmful scale.

The first step in confronting this problem is to recognise that it exists — that the potential is always there. Whether the potential is realised depends on many factors — some to do with the author, others to do with the subject — such as motive, understanding, and acceptance of what is being transacted, and issues of control in the relationship.

The second step is to recognise that there is a principle involved: we do not deliberately deceive people about what we are doing. The problem can present itself in small ways and in larger ways, but the principle remains equally important. It can present itself in a small way when, for example, we approach a bereaved family and ask if we can interview them about their loss. In order to persuade them, we might say we are writing a 'tribute' to the deceased person. This is a loose word, but it conveys a sense that the article will portray the deceased person in a generally positive light, and will emphasis achievements rather than shortcomings. It doesn't preclude us from including negative material, but we have implied that we will strike the balance in favour of the deceased. If instead we write a hatchet job, we have, of course, committed an act of betrayal. We have behaved unethically. On the other hand, if we are true to our word, and we write the kind of story we have led the family to expect, there is no betrayal.

The words of Sissela Bok come back to help us: we deceive when we encourage others to believe what we ourselves do not believe. If we have encouraged the family to believe that we are writing a 'tribute' and that is what we do, we have neither deceived nor betrayed. Much day-to-day journalism falls within this category. But much day-to-day journalism also confronts us with a related difficulty. This arises when we make an initial approach for an interview, believing in good faith that we are going to write a story that might be positive, or at least neutral, for the source, and then, as we gather more information, the story changes and becomes negative for the source. To publish this without going back to the source and giving him or her an opportunity to respond would be not only unfair but an act of betrayal. It follows that journalism does not necessarily involve betrayal, but the potential for this to occur is always there.

Some distinguished journalists take a more uncompromising view than this. In their view, betrayal is unavoidable. One such person is Michael Gawenda, a journalist with an outstanding career as a writer and foreign correspondent, and editor-in-chief of *The Age* for eight years. He has written and spoken publicly on this issue.[4] In the course of doing so, he recounted some episodes from his own career to illustrate how betrayal can occur. One clear example arose when, as a feature writer on *The Age*, he approached the chief commissioner of Victoria Police and asked if he could spend three weeks observing the police at work. He specifically asked if he could carry out this observation at Fitzroy police station. Fitzroy is an inner-northern suburb of Melbourne, and at the time had a relatively high proportion of Aboriginal residents. Gawenda had heard that the police at Fitzroy were racially prejudiced against Aboriginal people, and that they harassed and mistreated them. However, he said nothing of this to the chief commissioner. He just asked if he could have unfettered access to the police station in order to observe the officers at work. The chief commissioner agreed and took Gawenda personally to the station, where he introduced him and told the officers there of the arrangement.

In the weeks that followed, Gawenda came and went at all hours of the day and night. He sat quietly, never asking a question, never joining in conversations, never taking a note. After a while, the police forgot he was there. 'That was what I wanted. I wanted them to forget I was there,' he later said. Occasionally, an officer would stop and chat — about life, family, football — and sometimes an officer would confide in him about his frustrations or difficulties. But Gawenda never initiated these exchanges. He just listened. And as he listened he started to hear officers referring to Aboriginal people in highly racist terms. He had his story. When it was published, the officers at the police station were outraged. They felt betrayed, and they said so. The chief commissioner never said a word. In the event, a series of inquiries were established to investigate relations between Victoria Police and the Aboriginal community, and these in turn led to the creation of Aboriginal liaison officers in the force.

Gawenda's initial access to the police, based on his request to the chief commissioner, was gained by what might be called deception by omission. It was an omission he was conscious of at the time and that he honestly owned up to in discussing the case. At the same time, because of the policy changes that followed, perhaps some good came out of it. And there was never any question that the issue of racism in the police force was a matter of public interest. But this is an argument that says the ends justify the means, and Gawenda did not seek to defend his conduct on these grounds. He was adamant that all he wanted was a story. He got one — a big one — and the fact that some good might have come from it was no more than fortuitous.

It is, of course, perfectly possible that the chief commissioner, Mick Miller, who was an exceptionally strong and experienced leader, saw through Gawenda's initial request immediately. It is equally possible that he saw it as an opportunity to find out for himself what was really going on at Fitzroy and, at the same time, to generate external political pressure on the force that enabled him to make changes that he otherwise would have found more difficult. But Gawenda took care not to be upfront with him, in case he refused the request for access. It was in that act of omission and in his calculatedly unobtrusive behaviour while in the police station that the betrayal lay.

The ethical question left hanging in the air from this case is this: does 'getting the story' on its own constitute a justification for betrayal? If the answer to that is yes, then Janet Malcolm's argument is conclusively made out. If the answer is no, then her argument is not made out, but we have to take on the responsibility of finding an ethical justification for any betrayal we commit.

The question of betrayal is allied to another question: who 'owns' the story? Is it the journalist's or the subject's story? Journalists usually talk as if it is their story — 'my story got on the front page today' — and, of course, many times it is their story. They have constructed it from bits and pieces of evidence, or interviews or observations, and they have composed it using their own literary skills. But degrees of ownership of the story can vary with the circumstances.

For example, if we approach a subject on the basis they we are going to tell 'their story', that is an undertaking to be borne in mind when we come to write it. We have presented ourselves to the subject as a kind of vector by which 'their story' will be disseminated. Now, of course, we are not passive vectors like the seed-bearing wind. We are interventionist vectors. We choose the words, the structure, the order in which the story is constructed, and how we portray people. These choices are ours. That logically means that some part of the story is ours. But how much? How much of the story is 'theirs' when that is what we have said we will write?

This is more than just an academic point, because when we deal with traumatised people in the aftermath of a tragedy or disaster, sometimes their one objective in talking to us is to have their story told. When instead we decide to write 'our' story, this can lead to a sense of frustration and disillusionment in the subject. A survivor of the Black Saturday bushfires spoke about this. She and her husband had been picking over the ashes of their home, and had sat down to rest under a tree. A reporter had come up to her unexpectedly and said, 'You're being defiant.' (The reporter meant that the woman was taking a defiant stance in the face of the complete devastation of her home.) The subject replied, 'No, not really. We're just having lunch.' 'Oh no,' the reporter replied, 'you're being defiant.' Sure enough, the subject said, a story appeared in the next day's paper portraying them as defiant. 'She told her story,' the subject said of the reporter, 'not our story.' The reporter had asserted ownership of her story by choosing to portray the subject in a way that the subject had expressly disavowed. This is not deception, but it is betrayal of a kind. The subject had tolerated the reporter's approach, not wishing to be rude. No explicit undertakings had been given about how the story would be written, but to assert over the objection of the subject a particular form of portrayal was a breach of the implicit trust placed in the reporter by the subject in her preparedness to talk.

CHAPTER TWELVE
PRIVACY

Journalism and privacy are in fundamental conflict. Journalism is the means by which we act on behalf of the public in order to report to it. Privacy is the right to be *not* reported upon to the public. When we exercise the function of journalism in a way that violates that right, we require an ethical justification for doing so. We confront once more the now-familiar necessity to balance the public interest against a private interest. In this context, a good starting point for discussion is the libertarian philosophy of John Stuart Mill. In *On Liberty*, he wrote:

> The individual is not accountable to society for his actions, insofar as these concern the interests of no person but himself … For such actions as are prejudicial to the interests of others, the individual is accountable.[1]

This neatly captures the essence of the balancing required in journalism where privacy is at stake. Each person has the right to personal control over what he or she does, so long as it has no harmful effect on others. And if what he or she does has no harmful effects on others, what justification is there for us, in performing the public function of journalism, to intrude on them?

The idea of privacy has been expressed in many different ways, but one of the most enduring has been 'the right to be let alone' — a formulation devised by two American lawyers, Samuel Warren and Louis Brandeis. In 1890, they argued in an article in the *Harvard Law Review* for a legal remedy to protect individual privacy. They had been provoked to do this by the invasive behaviour of a newspaper towards Samuel Warren's family. In the *Review* article, they asserted the right of individuals 'to be let alone'. Brandeis was to use the same words 40 years later when, in a dissenting opinion on the United States Supreme Court, he opposed the right of the government to use evidence obtained by telephone-tapping or electronic eavesdropping. In a judgment that is still considered to be a landmark statement of principle, Justice Brandeis said:

> The makers of our Constitution ... sought to protect Americans in their beliefs, their thoughts, their emotions and their sensations. They conferred, as against the government, the right to be let alone — the most comprehensive of rights and the right most valued by civilized men.[2]

'The most comprehensive of rights and the right most valued by civilized man.' Strong language. And the argument is borne out by the status accorded to privacy in mankind's most universal legal instruments. Article 12 of the Universal Declaration of Human Rights, adopted by the United Nations in 1948, states that 'no one shall be subjected to arbitrary interference with his privacy, family, home or correspondence ...' The European Convention on Human Rights of 1950 (Article 8) and the International Covenant on Civil and Political Rights of 1966 (Article 17) are expressed in similar terms.

From these declarations, we can see immediately that privacy has several dimensions: personal life, family, home, and correspondence. Sissela Bok goes further. She describes privacy as the condition of being protected from unwanted access by others — either physical access, personal information, or attention.[3] These are much bigger and broader dimensions; but for them to have practical meaning for us in the work of journalism, some more specific constructs are needed.

At its core, something is private if it is an area of our lives over which we are entitled to absolute control, including particularly the right to control who else knows about it and how much they know. It is this area of our lives that is intimately bound up with our personal self, our inmost feelings, loves, desires, tendencies, thoughts, impulses, and beliefs.

From the legal instruments and Bok's broader conceptions, it is possible to specify at least seven domains of privacy, all of which are relevant to ethical decisions that we confront in journalism.

The first is the *personal* domain, which comprises:

- Details of our intimate relationships — the identity of the people those relationships are with, and what happens within those relationships.
- Our sexual orientation and proclivities.
- Our bodily functions.
- Details of our health — what disorders, if any, we have, and the treatments for them.
- Details of our financial arrangements.
- Our religious beliefs or lack of them.
- Our political beliefs and voting preferences.

There is an *emotional* domain. This is created out of our right to our dignity, where it might otherwise be stripped away by force of circumstance. The most common examples occur when we are traumatised or grieving. However, it might also occur in circumstances of great joy — for example, when we are reunited with someone we thought had been lost. In these circumstances, our emotions can overwhelm our self-control. When this happens, we are vulnerable and we may behave in ways that we would not normally behave, or do things in public that we would normally do only in private, if at all.

There is a *presentational* domain. It is part of our autonomy to decide how we appear in front of others. Depictions of us half-dressed in our bedroom, or ravaged by grief at a graveside, or when dead, are violations of this domain.

There is a *reputational* domain, which is separate from defamation. It arises, for example, from our right to rebuild our lives after a misfortune or disgrace without having the ashes of the past raked over. It may also arise over our right to keep private the fact that we have a health condition that implies moral turpitude such as a sexually transmissible disease. This is tempered by another person's right to know if his or her welfare has been placed at risk.

Then there is a *data* domain. This has been created by the accumulation of material about us that we have supplied for some particular purpose: financial information so we can obtain a bank loan or be assessed for taxation; medical information so we can get treatment; intimate information so we can get counselling.

And there is a *spatial* domain: our bedroom, the toilet, our house, our garden. What we do in those places we think of as private, partly because the places are physically separate and cloistered from public places, partly because we are entitled to enjoy there the rights of private property free from trespass or other unlawful intrusion, and partly because some of what we do in those places falls within the personal domain of privacy.

Finally, there is a *communications* domain: letters, emails, and telephone or personal conversations.

In the United States, the Supreme Court has recognised a legal right to 'survivor privacy' — the right of surviving family members to control personal information about deceased loved ones, for their own peace of mind.

All these domains and the rights that flow from them need to be recognised by us, and given due weight in our decisions about how to behave in gathering and in publishing material. The phrase 'due weight' introduces the next element in our decision-making.

The right to privacy, like the right to free speech and other civil rights, is not absolute. There are circumstances in which it gives way to wider or more pressing rights. In journalism, we are often called upon to strike a balance between an individual's interest in his or her privacy and the public interest in disclosure. Let us consider a range of circumstances in which this choice has to be made. We can use the modified Potter Box (chapter seven) and our public-interest test (chapter four) to help us make the choices in each case.

Public figures

While the codes of ethics do not pay much attention to this, the traditional media position in Australia is that when a person becomes a public figure, he or she forgoes some privacy, but does not forgo it all. The line is conventionally drawn at the place where private conduct, or relationships, or interests begin to impinge on the person's public duties. For example, if a government official is engaged in a sexual relationship with a person whose business interests the official has the power to advance or retard, the relationship clearly has the potential to improperly influence the official's public decision-making. On the other hand, if the relationship has no bearing on the person's public duties, the relationship is conventionally regarded as entirely private.

A relevant consideration is, who disclosed the information? If the public figure disclosed it, the right to privacy has been voluntarily waived. This occurred, for example, when Bob Hawke, as prime minister, revealed at a press conference that one of his daughters was a drug addict. The difficulty in that case, of course, was that Hawke breached not only his own privacy but his daughter's, and did so in circumstances where the media had no choice but to publish: he did it at a press conference that was carried live to a television audience.

However, this case raises a further question, concerning the relatives of public figures. To what extent, if at all, do the families of public figures forgo their personal privacy because of the public figure's position? Here are two more examples from real life in Australia.

- The son of a prime minister is suspended from his secondary school for his part in what one newspaper described as 'an alcohol-assisted scrape'. This boy was one of four involved in the incident, but was the only one named.
- The wife of a very senior public figure is charged with a minor shoplifting offence. The charge is subsequently found by a magistrate to have been validated, but he discharges her without conviction after hearing evidence in open court that she has been psychologically distressed.

Is there a justification for singling out the boy of the public figure for naming? Is there a justification for reporting on the shoplifting case? Might there be a context within which either of these could be reported in a way that added to the ethical case for reporting them?

Ordinary people caught up in news events

Many times, a judgment has to be made about the privacy interests of individuals caught up in news events that, by their nature, have a substantial public-interest element:

- A reporter who was present by chance when three daughters were told by their husbands that their parents had perished in the Black Saturday bushfires did not report what he saw and heard, but later interviewed one of the husbands and reported that interview.
- A newspaper withheld from publication a photograph of a man whose children had perished when a light plane crashed on their home near Essendon airport in Melbourne. The photograph was taken at the graveside as the white coffin of one of the children was being lowered. The father knelt at the head of the grave in a state of near collapse, supported under the arms by two friends, his face contorted with grief. It was a Melbourne newspaper that withheld the photo. However, a newspaper in Perth published it.

Celebrities

People who are famous for various reasons create special difficulties. Paul Chadwick, Victoria's founding privacy commissioner, developed a taxonomy of fame in which he identified five types:

1. Fame by election or appointment (what we have called public figures)
2. Fame by association (e.g. families of public figures)
3. Fame by chance (ordinary people caught up in news events)
4. Fame by being royal (members of the Royal Family and those who marry into it)

5. Fame by achievement (elite sportspeople, film stars, business leaders and the like)

Two more have emerged since Chadwick devised that list: fame by being famous (the Paris Hilton syndrome), and fame by Internet replication — the phenomenon of 'going viral'.

Let us deal with fame by being famous, because the balancing equation is different for them. These people live by publicity. For them, all publicity is good publicity, unless we get their names wrong. But might there be limits to what we could ethically publish, even for these people? The answer is, of course, yes. They may not be the only interested party in the equation. The privacy of their partners, children, and parents can be invaded incidentally.

The Royal Family is also a difficult case because of its constitutional position. It follows that statements made or behaviour engaged in by its members or hangers-on that affect the public standing or attitudes towards the Royal Family may have a public-interest element. The closer the involvement of the Queen, as head of state, or the immediate heir, the Prince of Wales, the greater the public-interest element is likely to be because of their constitutional significance. For example, there was a legitimate public interest in Prince Charles's re-marriage, because he will probably become king of Australia, and his spouse will become either queen or consort. However, it is difficult to see the public interest in publishing details of his explicit and intimate longings for her conveyed in private correspondence and leaked to the media.

Somewhat more clear-cut is the position with regard to those who have gained fame by achievement. Where a private matter affects their public performance, there is a public-interest element. That is why publishing details of sporting injuries suffered by sporting figures is uncontroversial, even though medical conditions generally are regarded as part of the personal domain of privacy. Note, however, the term 'sporting' injuries. Other medical conditions do not so easily acquire public-interest status.

In August 2007, a Melbourne commercial television station, Channel 7, published medical records of two Australian Football League (AFL) players, showing they were being treated for drug addiction.

There were many ethical questions in that case. The first concerned how the records were obtained. They were said to have been found in the street outside a rehabilitation centre. Does that sound plausible? *Two* sets of records? What steps needed to be taken to establish that they had not been unlawfully obtained? If they had, what was the station's ethical — not to say legal — duty? Even if the account of how they had become available was true, did that make them public? What else might the finder have done with them?

Second, there was the question of payment. Channel 7 paid the finder for the material.

Third, what was the public interest in publishing the material? The channel claimed its story would 'lift the lid on drug use in a Melbourne football club'. The channel also argued that AFL players were role models and that they needed to be 'kept honest'. The channel argued that these reasons overrode the players' right to privacy and the breaching of doctor–patient confidentiality.

Fourth was the question of identifying the players. The channel decided not to name them, but did want to name their club. However, this was forestalled by a court injunction preventing them from doing so.

Finally, there was the question of verification. The following exchange is taken from a transcript of an interview on the ABC-TV program *Media Watch* between Channel 7's director of news and current affairs, Peter Meakin, and the program's interviewer, Monica Attard:

> *Meakin*: Well, he [the Channel 7 reporter] made the effort to contact the clinic, the referring doctor, the counsellor involved, and most of those calls went unreturned, as I understand. But a number of people pored over the documents, including our legal people, and they appeared to be genuine, so we published them in good faith.
>
> *Attard*: Did Channel 7, do you think, do enough to establish the circumstances of how these documents were actually obtained?
>
> *Meakin*: Well, we were told they'd been found in the street. That may well be the case. We do not know that they were stolen. We know that someone's been charged with the rather unusual offence of theft by finding, um, but I don't know whether they were stolen.

Does that indicate rigorous inquiry? Medical records are deeply personal, and so are doctor–patient consultations. The public-interest justification for breaching them, therefore, needs to be proportionally high. Does Channel 7's 'role model' argument reach this threshold? As for its 'lift the lid' argument, there was already information in the public domain that at least 20 AFL players had tested positive to drugs.

Business leaders may also achieve fame by achievement. While their personal financial affairs also fall within the domain of personal privacy, they may justifiably be required to yield relevant parts of that privacy in the public interest if credible allegations are made about their behaviour — for example, about a possible financial conflict of interest. This applies as much to business journalists as anyone else, incidentally. The test always starts with these questions:

- What is the public interest in disclosing this information?
- What is the nature and extent of likely harm to be caused?
- Who will suffer?
- Is the public interest to be served proportional to the harm?
- If there is a public interest in publishing, how can the harm be minimised?

In making this assessment, we also need to consider the privacy domain involved. All the domains are important, and cannot be put in a hierarchy. However, the more intimate the information, the higher the public-interest threshold becomes. In the case of the footballers whose medical records were published, it is incontrovertible that medical records are part of the personal domain of privacy, and that they concern intimate details of the individual. It is therefore among the most private of information. The public-interest threshold needing to be surmounted is correspondingly high.

Privacy as an ethical constraint

In Australia, there is no general right to sue for breaches of privacy. There are limited ways to take action against governments and corporations for breaches of the privacy laws, but these are narrow, and confined generally to data use, data management, and data sharing. In March 2014, the Australian Law Reform Commission published a discussion paper recommending the creation of a tort of privacy in Australian law. This would give people the right to sue and recover damages for 'serious' breaches of privacy. The commission's proposals follow a number of important legal cases in England and Australia, indicating that the courts are moving in this direction already. The House of Lords and the English Court of Appeal have suggested that, in certain circumstances what has been hitherto thought of as the ancient legal doctrine of breach of confidence might now be thought of as a breach of privacy.[4] Following this line of analysis, the then chief justice of the High Court of Australia, Justice Murray Gleeson, stated in a judgment involving the Australian Broadcasting Corporation, 'The foundation of much of what is protected, where rights of privacy, as distinct from rights of property, are acknowledged, is human dignity.'

He then formulated a test of what is private:

> Disclosure or observation of information or conduct [which] would be highly offensive to a reasonable person of ordinary sensibilities is in many cases a useful practical test of what is private.[5]

Not very long after this, the ABC broadcast on three successive radio news bulletins increasingly explicit information about a woman whose husband had been convicted of raping her. The information included her name. She sued the ABC for breach of statutory duty, negligence, breach of confidence, and invasion of privacy, and succeeded on all four grounds.

Judge Felicity Hampel, in the Victorian County Court, following the House of Lords' line of reasoning, held that confidence may be breached where the information is such 'in respect of which a person has a reasonable expectation of privacy' and where that information was published in circumstances where the publisher knew or ought to have known of that reasonable expectation of privacy.[6]

Judge Hampel held that the information in question was easy to identify as private, being of a sexual nature. She also held (in addition to finding a breach of confidence) that the relevant breach of privacy was 'an actionable wrong which gives rise to a right to recover damages according to the ordinary principles governing damages in tort'. In other words, this was a wrong that the plaintiff was entitled to sue and recover damages for. She determined that it was an appropriate case to respond, although cautiously, to the invitation held out by Justice Gleeson in the High Court in the earlier action involving the ABC. She awarded damages of more than $234,000 against the ABC. This specifically included damages for invasion of privacy.

The ABC considered appealing to the High Court, but did not do so. It is reasonable to suppose that this decision was based at least partly on concern that if they did appeal, the court would make good on its previous warning and confirm the existence of a tort of privacy in respect of persons. Since then, there have been other cases which indicate that the Victorian Supreme Court has not followed Judge Hampel. However, the *obiter dictum* of Justice Gleeson still hangs poised over the media, and might come down like a sword of Damocles if the circumstances of a case happen to fit the Gleeson criteria.

CHAPTER THIRTEEN
TRAUMA, DISASTERS, AND SUICIDE

Covering disasters and suicide presents many acute ethical difficulties in journalism because of the risk that, in trying to do our job, we will do *unanticipated* and *unintentional* harm to others, particularly to traumatised people. This confronts us with a completely different situation from the one we face when we have to strike a balance between meeting our public-interest obligations and doing *anticipated* harm. We are responsible for anticipated harm frequently; but when this happens as a consequence of fulfilling our obligations to the community, it is ethically justifiable to do so. For example, when we report proceedings from the criminal courts, there can be no question that publicity, at least initially, harms the accused person, since it conveys to the world that he or she is suspected of a crime. But it can also harm witnesses, either when they give highly emotional testimony (thus publicly exposing their grief), or when their truthfulness is questioned by barristers.

When we cover disasters or suicide, however, we might do harm without even knowing we are doing it. What we do know is that people caught up in these events will be traumatised. That is our starting point. When we cover suicide — either as an issue of public interest, or in a specific case where someone has taken his or her own life — there is a risk that we will add to the grief of the bereaved, that we will increase the risk of copycat behaviours, and that we will legitimise the act of suicide. When we cover disasters, there is a risk that we will add to the trauma of already traumatised people. This risk can arise in several ways: by having them revisit experiences that they do not wish to revisit; by probing for an emotional response and thereby bringing their grief to the surface publicly; by intruding on their grief; or by portraying them in a vulnerable state. Experiences like this can set back their psychological recovery.

We need to have a basic understanding of the psychology of trauma if we are to be able to minimise these risks. Trauma affects people in many different ways. Some become hyperactive — running around, attending to everyone else's needs, talking incessantly, trying to exert some control over the situation. Some become visibly distressed — crying, distraught, confused. Some are numbed, immobile, unable to think clearly, while others cope by switching off, becoming silent and withdrawn.

It is in the coverage of disasters and suicide, then, that the value of responsibility as referred to in the codes of ethics is paramount. We have a responsibility to minimise these risks, and we give ourselves the best chance of minimising harm if we act responsibly. But what does this mean in practical terms? To answer this question, we need to look in detail at each of these areas.

Disasters

There is a clear public interest in disasters being reported. They have a devastating effect on communities; the public needs to know what happened and why, so as to minimise the risk of a recurrence; victims and survivors need a voice so they can tell their stories and feel that their part in the disaster is recognised and legitimised; there is a need to rally public assistance; and there is a need to hold to account those who may not have adequately discharged their responsibilities for preventing or responding to the disaster.

It follows from this that an important part of reporting on a disaster includes gathering the accounts of survivors, since they are among the strongest witnesses. And what happened to them is ultimately part of a larger story, which is likely to include issues of blame and causation — both in themselves matters of public interest.

What follows is based on research carried out among survivors of the Black Saturday bushfires in Victoria, and among the journalists who covered the fires.[1]

The first ethical issue to arise for journalists dealing with survivors was the question of consent. As discussed in chapter eight, the concept of 'informed' consent, in the sense that people give careful consideration to an approach from the media, is an impossible standard to apply in the immediate aftermath of a disaster. Survivors are in such a state of shock and disorientation that they cannot possibly give informed consent; even simple consent is not feasible. Instead, survivors rely on their instincts, and what feeds into that instinctual response comes down to the answer to this internal question: *Is this person respecting my autonomy?*

In addition to this question of survivor autonomy, there was a further important factor for journalists to consider when dealing with people in the aftermath of the disaster: the timing of the encounter. Many survivors said that in the first 48 hours or so after the fires, they were on an extreme adrenaline 'high'. Symptoms of this included hyperactivity — running around doing chores, looking after other people, talking all the time — or a sense of invincibility or euphoria. Several survivors spoke of being 'out of touch with reality' or 'a bit whacko', or of feeling 'able to go ten rounds with Mike Tyson' [a world-champion boxer].

Despite their upbeat appearances, these people were, in fact, in a state of shock and disorientation. Later, many could not remember in very much detail what had happened during this time. Their testimony revealed that they did not really comprehend what they were doing or saying. Some did not even make the connection between speaking to a reporter and seeing themselves in a newspaper or on television. Some were surprised at what they had said in the interview — they had not realised they had given away so much detail. Some needed to spill out the most grisly details of what they had seen or how their loved ones had died.

The vulnerability revealed by this evidence means that there is an especially high ethical responsibility on us to understand the emotional state that survivors of a disaster are in, and to treat them accordingly. Our ethical responses govern not only how we should approach survivors and what questions to ask, but what we should select for publication and the way in which we portray them. In deciding these questions, we might ask ourselves, *How much detail does my audience need in order to understand what has happened? Am I portraying this person in a way that respects their dignity? Have I done all I can to minimise the risk of harm?*

After about the first 48 hours or so of a disaster, survivors' attitudes to the media change. This has been observed both by media practitioners and survivors, as well as by clinicians in the field. There are several reasons for this. While adrenalin levels often remain at abnormally high levels for weeks, they are no longer sufficient to stem the rising tide of grief that accompanies the realisation of what has happened. With this comes a change in their attitude to the media. Essentially, they no longer have needs that the media can meet. They no longer have the urgent need or desire to tell their story that they felt in the immediate aftermath. They do not regard follow-up stories as having the same 'news' legitimacy as the initial stories about the disaster itself — in fact, they are more likely to see follow-up stories as exploitative, especially when we want to explore the disaster's impact on their emotions.

This change of mood has many consequences for us. We can no longer take it for granted that survivors will be willing to speak to us; the chance of a refusal, perhaps even an angry refusal, increases. As well, it is accompanied by a change to the type of questioning that is acceptable to survivors. Experienced reporters know this. One said, 'I knew we couldn't ask the same questions two or three days later that we would have been able to ask immediately after the fires.' As a matter of clinical fact, this is a very important point. Asking survivors days later to re-visit their experiences during the disaster can cause serious psychological harm. We must not do this under any circumstances. We should let survivors tell us what happened if they want to, but we should not probe for this or for more detail than the survivors volunteer. We should ask only enough questions to clarify something already said. On no account — at any stage — should we say, 'How do you feel?' or 'I understand how you feel.' Questions or comments such as these betray a lack of empathy, and can provoke anger.

At this stage, many survivors are focused on the present — what is happening to them now — and on the future — what are they going to do? Many have put the horror of the recent past into a part of their minds where they can revisit it as they feel able to, but that time is probably not now. It is one of the skills of trauma psychologists to able to help survivors with this process. We are not trauma psychologists, so it is trespassing into dangerous territory if we ask survivors to revisit their pain for our benefit. We should ask, instead, about their present situation and what their needs are. They will then tell us what they want to tell us.

One of the most difficult issues to deal with in the aftermath of any disaster is how to respond if a survivor breaks down. Our first response should be an offer to stop, to let the survivor compose himself. Usually, this is enough. It takes the pressure off the survivor, and he will resume almost straight away. However, if it becomes obvious that the distress is not going to abate, we should offer to withdraw: 'Would you like to stop now?' If the survivor says yes, we should ask whether he would prefer us to use or not to use the material gathered to that point. It is in these ways that we place as much control of the encounter as possible in the hands of the survivor. It is in these ways that we show we recognise and respect the survivor's autonomy.

However, simply because a person is crying is not a reason to avoid approaching them. It is a matter of degree. If a person is transported with grief, clearly an approach would be wrong. But people who are visibly upset are likely to be demonstrating a healthy association with what is going on, and may be considered to be coping reasonably well. It is not uncommon for survivors to agree to have their crying depicted because there is an authenticity about it: 'That is how I was.' However, what is absolutely unacceptable from an ethical point of view is to attempt to provoke survivors to tears, as this can potentially embarrass and enrage them. In their already-fragile state, embarrassment and anger do them further harm, and it is harm for which there is no justification.

Great caution is required, however, when people are in what appears to be a trance-like state. So far from demonstrating a healthy association with what is going on, these people are showing symptoms of what psychologists call dissociation.

This is a psychological defence-mechanism, which consists of shutting out the present reality while the person finds a way to confront it. Breaking into that state wrenches the person back into the present, forcing him or her to confront what has happened at a time when he or she is psychologically ill-prepared to do so. This can cause harm by increasing their trauma and perhaps delaying their long-term recovery. A good rule of thumb is that if we see a person in a trance-like state — gazing into space, seemingly disconnected from other people or from what is going on — we should leave them alone. They may not be showing any other outward signs of shock or grief, but they are particularly vulnerable.

It is paramount when writing the story that we keep in mind the vulnerable state of the people we have seen and spoken to. This is a circumstance when we should make it 'their' story first, and 'ours' second. We must absolutely keep faith with any promises we have made about the type of story we are writing, take pains to be fair in how we portray people, and avoid gratuitous grisly detail.

We also need to be accurate. Even small inaccuracies are regarded by traumatised people as major betrayals, with adverse consequences for their state of mind and recovery. A reporter who covered the Black Saturday fires recounted how, in writing about a family's experience, he had got the model of the family car wrong — not the make, but the model. Rationally speaking, in the great scheme of things, this was a trivial error. However, traumatised people are not in a rational state. The family member the reporter had interviewed rang him up in a rage because of the mistake. He spoke to her for a long time, and eventually she congratulated him on the overall quality of the story and of his coverage in general. But it showed how important accuracy is in these circumstances.

Suicide

We would not usually report how a person has died unless there were public-interest reasons for doing so. The circumstances and causes of most deaths are private — unless there is a powerful reason to reveal them. For example, deaths caused by a disaster commonly become public because of the general public interest in knowing about the disaster, its consequences, and its causes. Deaths caused by accidents or workplace hazards are public deaths, too, either because they take place in public or because the causative factors are a matter of public interest. For example, the deaths of three young men who were electrocuted while installing roof insulation as part of a federal government program in 2009 and 2010 were public because they revealed shortcomings in the way this taxpayer-funded program had been rolled out.

The difficulty with suicides, however, is that they can be public or private depending on a variety of circumstances. One such circumstance is the degree of public exposure and interest that the death itself creates. For example, if a person jumps off a busy bridge during peak hour, and extensive traffic disruption ensues, there is a public-interest justification in reporting this event because the public is entitled to an explanation for the disruption. Another circumstance may be that the suicide is evidence of a systemic failure or stress that the public has an interest in knowing about. For example, there was an extensive public debate in Victoria in the early 2000s about the stress on principals of government schools. In the midst of this debate, a principal took his own life. His death was reported in the context of the wider debate, and it caused the debate to intensify.

There also have been extensive public debates about youth suicide, suicides among asylum-seekers, and suicides among Aboriginal people in custody. All these are real matters of public interest, and to ignore or suppress the incidences of such deaths would be to keep the community in ignorance of a serious aspect of the associated problems and their causes.

Another circumstance arises when someone who has taken their own life had such a high public profile that their death-by-suicide cannot be ignored, and the events surrounding it cannot be glossed over. The death in Cape Town in November 2011 of the renowned and widely admired cricket commentator Peter Roebuck was an example of this. The death of a public figure such as Roebuck was a matter of genuine public interest, and not mere public curiosity. In addition, his death occurred while he was being questioned by police over a sexual-assault allegation.

Against any such public-interest considerations, we do, however, need to weigh the harm or risk of harm that our reporting might do.

Harm can be done to the bereaved families and friends of the deceased by the mere fact of reporting that a death was the result of suicide. The fact that someone died by their own hand is always a distressing disclosure because, in the aftermath of many suicides, those closest to the deceased person commonly experience feelings of guilt, remorse, and shame. These are hard enough to deal with in private, but the distress can be magnified significantly if the fact becomes public.

So before reporting a death by suicide, we need to ask ourselves whether there is a public interest — not just public curiosity — in our reporting it as such. There are, after all, strong arguments against running stories about suicide. When they involve a celebrity, there is plenty of evidence that such reports can lead to copycat deaths by vulnerable or suggestible people who think that because a celebrity has taken their life, there is some sort of glamour attached to it, or that it is somehow an acceptable way out. And in some cases a death that may appear to be suicide may later prove to be accidental or unintentional. Speculative statements by the police about the nature of a death may be unreliable. It is better to use a formulation such as, 'Police say there are no suspicious circumstances', or 'Police say there is no evidence of foul play', rather than to explicitly refer to suicide. The death might turn out to be accidental, and the actual cause may not be confirmed until an inquest has been held.

Let us look in more depth at these considerations. First, how prevalent is the copycat problem? A study in Australia in 2001 concluded that there is an association between news portrayals of suicides and subsequent suicides, and that in some cases this association is likely to be causal.[2] Other research led to the conclusion that the greater the amount of media coverage on suicide, the greater the suicide rate, especially if celebrity suicides or actual suicides were reported in newspapers.[3]

In the face of evidence like this, it is an ethical imperative for us to be cautious in the way we deal with stories on this subject. If we have decided that there is a public interest in reporting a death as suicide, we need to ask ourselves two more questions. How sure are we that it was suicide? And how much detail is it necessary to publish in order to meet our duty to the public interest? Best practice and advice from clinicians in the field indicates that reports should avoid dramatic language or images, avoid stating the location, avoid stating the method used, and provide accurate facts about causes of death, including due emphasis on any mental-health problems.[4]

In the Roebuck case, there was ample first-hand evidence that the cricket commentator was in a despairing frame of mind just before he died. By drawing attention to this, the media reports of his death provided an essential context for it. Many media reports also used the word 'fell' to describe what occurred, as this is a neutral, passive word that is less dramatic than alternatives such as 'jumped' or 'leaped'.

Vocabulary is important here, because it is essential to keep in mind the effect of what is being published on emotionally vulnerable people. The Commonwealth government has put out an educational kit designed to help the media negotiate this difficult terrain. It says, in part:

> People in despair are often unable to identify solutions to their problems, and may be influenced by what they read, see or hear. The effect may be more profound if someone feels able to identify with the person who died, perhaps because they are in the same age group or share similar experiences or ideals. An explicit report, particularly one which provides details about the method of self-harm, may lead those who are vulnerable to take a similar course of action.[5]

This reminds us that when we are making decisions on this topic, we need to take into account not just the effect on an ordinary person, or even on the family and friends of the deceased, but the effect on emotionally vulnerable people. That is an unusual but obviously necessary test. Our usual ethical assessment involves balancing a private interest with the general public interest. Here, though, the general public interest is not monolithic. The public, in this case, includes categories of people who are mentally ill, suggestible, or vulnerable in some other way, and we need to take the avoidance-of-harm approach. This means taking their well-being into account, too, when deciding whether and how to report suicide.

The evidence also suggests that, as part of this harm-minimisation process, it is recommended that the contact details of help lines and support services of organisations such as Lifeline and beyondblue be provided, so that people who are vulnerable or at risk may obtain help.

CHAPTER FOURTEEN

ONLINE ETHICAL PROBLEMS

While the values and principles that guide us in giving effect to the ethics of journalism are enduring, technology can alter the guise in which ethical dilemmas appear. This is certainly true of digital technology. As increasing amounts of journalism are being conducted online, the new guises in which old ethical problems appear are multiplying. Moreover, a number of ethical problems arise in online journalism that do not arise at all in conventional journalism — or else they add new elements to old ethical questions. The 'old' areas particularly affected are truth-telling (especially verification); impartiality; taste and decency; and privacy and consent.

The 'new' areas are participation, or 'the news conversation'; and rights of ownership.

Our starting point, however, is that whatever changes are wrought by technology, the values and principles that underpin the ethics of journalism remain constant, because they are grounded in the moral philosophies on which our society is built. These transcend technology and methods of communication, although their practical application may differ.

Verification

Verifying the accuracy of material *before* its publication has been the first requirement of conventional journalism. This was important enough when — in the era of what we think of now as 'heritage media' — the sources of news were relatively few. Now, the existence of so many more sources of information brought into being by the Internet makes it even more important that those wishing to engage in journalism verify their material prior to publication. The reason is obvious: the task for the ordinary citizen in sifting informational gold from informational dross has got exponentially more difficult. When the information world is awash with vast amounts of material undifferentiated as to reliability and accuracy, public discourse suffers. It becomes hostage to rumour, gossip, and innuendo.

Because those who engage in journalism enter into an implicit social contract with the community to provide accurate and reliable information that can be depended upon as having been assessed and filtered by reference to the established norms of professional journalism, an ethical obligation raises its head to assert the need for prior verification.

Matt Drudge, the blogger behind the *Drudge Report* in the United States, has acknowledged that only about 80 per cent of his factual material had been verified before publication. The rest was rumour and gossip. The question for his audience is: which 80 per cent? Once material is published, it is on the public record, rightly or wrongly, corrected or not corrected, and available to anyone to pick up and pass on. This is not a standard that is acceptable as journalism.

Failure to verify can lead to our being duped by hoaxers and fraudsters. In January 2013, Jonathan Moylan, an anti-coalmining activist, issued a fake media release, using a forged letterhead of the ANZ bank, headed: 'ANZ divests from

Maules Creek project'. It purported to announce that the ANZ bank had withdrawn a \$1.2 billion loan facility to Whitehaven Coal, 'which was primarily intended for the Maules Creek Coal Project'. It quoted Toby Kent, who was described as the ANZ Group Head of Corporate Sustainability. A phone number for Kent was provided. When journalists rang this number, it was answered by Jonathan Moylan, pretending to be Kent.

The Australian Financial Review and Australian Associated Press posted the fake announcement on their online news services. Within 25 minutes, \$314 million was wiped off the Whitehaven share price, whereupon the Australian Securities and Investments Commission halted trading in the shares. After the hoax was revealed and the stories retracted, trading resumed, and the share price recovered to close fractionally up on the day.

A further challenge to verification has appeared with smartphone-based photo and video-making technology. There have been many instances where media outlets have re-broadcast this material, taking it at face value. For example, in 2013, during the civil war in Syria, propaganda videos were circulated by both sides claiming to show atrocities being committed by the other. One piece of footage showed a person being beheaded with a chainsaw; however, later reports stated that this atrocity had occurred five years previously in Mexico. And footage alleged to show Syrian government forces beating prisoners was later revealed to have been taken in Lebanon four years previously. Caution is needed in selecting such material for re-publication, and in seeing that any necessary caveats about verification are published with it.

Particular caution is required where large and complex data are concerned, where the risks of serious harm may be high, and where our knowledge of the risks is limited. In these cases, such as with WikiLeaks, a conservative approach to disclosure is ethically preferable to an adventurous approach, because of the risk of serious harm.

Impartiality

The demand for impartiality in conventional journalism rests in part on the fact that in heritage media there are limits of time and space, thereby forcing journalists to select and omit information so that the story fits. Considerations of impartiality, especially fairness and balance, play into that selection process. Online platforms, however, do not have such physical limitations. Instead, they are limited by what might be called journalists' bandwidths — the constant pressure to file and update stories, while having little time to get across the vast amount of available material in a way that allows us to make informed judgments about what to put in and what to leave out.

As online journalists, in addition to having to decide what to include in or exclude from our copy, we must now also make decisions about what hyperlinks to insert — and our choices about this are now part of the test of our impartiality. If we insert links that represent a spectrum of principal relevant perspectives on the story, we are likely to be judged to have passed this test. If we insert only those links that present a particular viewpoint on the issue, we are likely to be judged to have failed the test.

This is a good and relevant test, because hyperlinks allow readers to enter a story at different points, and to explore some aspects in far greater depth than would ordinarily be available through a conventional media report. This is a great advantage for the reader; to deny him or her a fair opportunity to take it, by a skewed or incomplete provision of hyperlinks, is a failure of impartiality.

The professional duty here is captured in a clause of a code of ethics for online journalism developed by the Canadian Broadcasting Company:

- We enrich the experience of our online users by providing links from our news stories to other sites.
- The links reflect the pertinent views on an issue. Links should reflect the journalistic principle of balance.
- We take care that the sites we link to are legally sound, and we take into consideration matters of taste.
- We give users enough information about the site we are linking to so they have some basis for deciding whether they wish to follow the link.[1]

Content-linking also presents ethical challenges that are unique to online journalism. Linking our audience to content on other sites has no exact parallel in conventional journalism, because even though conventional journalists can refer their audiences to other sources such as reports, books, articles, and electronic-data records, each of these generally will have been subject to some quality control in its own right.

That is not necessarily the case with websites. Unless we know and can vouch for the content of the other site, or it comes with a reputation we can reasonably rely on, referring our audience on is a risk for which we can be held accountable ethically. It implies an endorsement by us, even if we don't intend it to be. So we have a responsibility — to ourselves as much as to anyone else — to thoroughly acquaint ourselves with any content to which we are linking people. What criteria might we use in selecting our hyperlinks? Here are some:

- *Reliability* Do we have good reason to trust that the content on the linked website is likely to be accurate?

- *Expertise* Does the provider of the link have genuine expertise?
- *Independence* Do we have any reason to doubt the independence of the provider?
- *Freshness* How recently was the website updated, or might it be out of date?
- *Quality of factual content* Is the material factually substantive and unambiguously written?
- *Informativeness* What is the ratio of factual content to comment?

And if we, as journalists, see on someone's website a claim to be expert in some field or other, is it acceptable for us then to use that in a news story without verifying whether the claim to expertise is true? Is it even enough to say a person claims on his or her website to be an expert? In assessing this, we need to take into account the impressionistic way in which people absorb news. They do not read the fine print, so a word like word 'expert' jumps out of the text. It is easy to convey a misleading impression while at the same time protecting ourselves with fine print.

Taste and decency

Journalism has always required a judgment to be made about how much offensive, intrusive, or sickening material needs to be included in order to convey to the audience a sufficient understanding of what has happened. Digital technologies, especially those provided by cameras and videos, combined with instant-broadcast capability, have presented many new challenges here. Material is publicly available now that would never have got beyond the television producer's cutting room or the photographic editor's desk in the past. Indeed, many professional camera operators or photographers would not have shot much of this material in the first place, knowing that their judgment would be called into question by their superiors.

Such gate-keeping does not occur in the digital world, so a lot of this kind of material is now available. But does availability in itself justify re-publication? The ethical answer is no. If material is offensive, intrusive, or sickening, we need a justification for publishing it, based on the criterion of the audience's need to know.

For example, in the immediate aftermath of the Boston Marathon bombing in April 2013, large quantities of such material were broadcast on the Internet. It was noticeable that the websites of the established news organisations such as *The Boston Globe* carried fewer graphic images, and fewer identifying images, than did websites not run by established media outlets. Among the images broadcast by those other websites was a photograph of a man in a wheelchair showing the lower half of his left leg blown off. The bloodied mass of torn flesh and the remnant shinbone were clearly visible, since the photo had been taken from directly in front and at short range. The man's face, also clearly identifiable, was a study in shock.

Arguments can be made for publishing this, of course. One would be that it demonstrates the harsh reality of the destruction and life-changing injury caused by acts of terrorism. The counter-argument would be: can this be demonstrated without such intrusive and sickening detail? Choices like this are much more common in the digital world than they were in the pre-digital one.

Privacy and consent

Many people place pictures and information about themselves on social-networking sites, and some journalists now routinely take this material and publish it. Some make an attempt to contact the person first and obtain permission to do so, but many take the view that dealing with content like this is akin to dealing with entries in *Who's Who*: people have chosen to go public with this information about themselves, and therefore it is available without restriction for use by journalists.

There is a difficulty with this position. It is a fundamental principle of privacy — enshrined in all Australian and many international privacy laws — that material made available for one purpose may not be used for another purpose without the consent of the provider. Many data-matching laws are based on this principle. For example, taxpayers are obliged to provide the Tax Office with details of their income for the purpose of having their tax liability assessed. The Tax Office may not pass on that information to a credit-worthiness agency without the taxpayer's consent, although it may pass it on to Centrelink if the taxpayer seeks to claim a benefit (and this capability is clearly stated in the Tax Act).

So, for example, if someone puts up a picture of themselves taken at a party, when they are perhaps slightly the worse for wear, for the purpose of sharing their social experience with their friends, is it right that it should be downloaded without consent to accompany a story about the death of their parents?

A further aspect of privacy online is the question of 'lurking'. Is lurking in a chat room — that is, seeing and recording the exchange for journalistic purposes, without divulging who we are and what we are doing — akin to eavesdropping? If it is, how does that fit in with the principle that we should declare to our subjects what we are doing? What use, if any, might or should we make of the information? Should we not use it at all unless it meets the public-interest test we set for ourselves in considering whether it is justified to invade someone's privacy, as discussed in chapter twelve? If it does meet that test, might we use the material just as a lead or a cue for getting further information using honest means? Or might we use the material as publishable content?

In 2009, the Australian Broadcasting Corporation published a guidance note to its editorial staff concerning the use in news reports of pictures retrieved from social-networking sites.[2] It makes the important general point that while sites such as Facebook and Myspace contain pictures that are public spaces in some ways, in other ways 'they are private to varying degrees'. It then lists six factors to be considered by staff who are contemplating using these pictures in news reports. The six are:

1. What was the person's reasonable expectation about the extent to which the picture would be disseminated? For example, is it obvious from the context that the person intended it to be fully available to the public? Was the picture posted by the person themselves or someone else? Were there any conditions attached to the wider use of the picture?
2. Can the person's consent be obtained?
3. If not, does the public interest in using the picture outweigh the person's reasonable expectation concerning privacy, and the impact that publication may have on the person themselves or anyone else who happens to be in the picture, taking into account that the person may be suffering grief or distress?
4. What steps have been taken to verify the picture?
5. Have relevant legal issues such as copyright, defamation, or contempt of court been taken into account?

6. Would the context in which it proposed to use the picture be likely to humiliate or otherwise do harm disproportionate to the public interest to be served?

Participation or 'the news conversation'

Journalism is no longer about the few transmitting material to the many, but about the many exchanging material among the many. This has made real the concept of the 'marketplace of ideas' that John Milton and John Stuart Mill wrote about centuries ago but could not have imagined would be so big and open.

The online journalist has a new role here, different from that of the conventional journalist: that of facilitator or host. Once confined to radio and television, this function is now part of the wider conception of what it means to be a journalist. It brings new responsibilities, too: whom to include and whom to exclude, and why; selecting what subjects will be debated; and making judgments about the language in which the debate will occur, and the boundaries to be set.

To take an unpalatable yet plausible example: imagine we are debating measures to restrict access to child pornography, and a participant begins to offer explicit details of the kind of material he or she has seen. What do we do? Where do we draw the line? If, in our judgment, the debate has moved into an exchange of perverted experiences, do we just sit there and let it happen, or do we have a responsibility as a host or facilitator to step in and put a stop to it? It is another case of an old question — editing or censorship? — in a new guise.

As discussed in chapter four, the answer lies in establishing motive and intention. We need to ask, *Why am I shutting this down or cutting this out, and what do I hope to achieve by doing so? What might be the consequences if I fail to act?*

Rights of ownership

As people engaged in journalism, what rights do we have to promote one set of interests over another? If we are running our own digital platform, we have proprietorial rights and the power to do as we please. How ought we balance these rights of ownership with our journalistic ethical duties when the two collide? A useful way is to apply the principles of editorial independence discussed in chapter six. The essence of such independence is that journalistic decisions should be made on the basis of news values and other relevant considerations, and not on the basis of self-interest, commercial advantage, or an improper motive such as revenge.

Of course, as an owner we have the right to express our opinion. How we do so is not just a matter of ethics, but also one of credibility. If we write in a way that suppresses inconvenient facts, or distorts the facts, or is an *ad hominem* rave (an attack on someone as a person) rather than an attack on an argument, we will lose credibility as well as expose ourselves as unethical.

One great benefit of making professional decisions on the basis of values and principles is that, while the circumstances may change, the values and principles are enduring. So if we take the trouble to think about and practise them, they can provide guidance in unfamiliar surroundings, or in the fog of uncertainty, or in the blind rush of events.

CHAPTER FIFTEEN

TAKING CARE OF OURSELVES

So far, the discussion in this book has been largely about our ethical duties to others. However, we also have an ethical duty to care for ourselves, which we owe not just to ourselves as individuals, but also to our families and friends. Journalism is a demanding profession, and people who pursue it — whether as employees of an organisation or as individuals — tend to select into it, and those who are not suited tend to select out. Those who select in are, on the whole, a resilient lot. However, this has led to the development of an unfortunate culture in which it is seen as a weakness to show emotion, or to confess to finding it hard to cope. In other words, 'real reporters don't cry'. Well, in fact they do, and they would not be human if they didn't. In the research about journalists who covered the Black Saturday bushfires, most of the respondents became emotional at some point during their interviews with the researchers, and that was six months after the event.

The culture, though, militates against their showing emotion in front of their colleagues, especially their superiors. Media organisations operated for decades — centuries — on the basis that journalism was a tough caper, and that if you weren't tough enough to do it, that was your own lookout. The results were seen in high incidences of alcohol abuse, nervous breakdowns, and marital failures. Some companies established trusts or foundations to help out employees and their families when a crisis struck. The Fairfax Foundation, for example, supported the families of many employees who fell prey to the pressures, by paying their mortgages or putting their children through school. But all this took place after the damage was done. Prevention was simply not part of the thinking.

This is changing, but slowly and unevenly. Most journalists who covered the Black Saturday bushfires did not generally accept offers by their employers to undergo counselling, for fear that their cards would be marked — that they would not in future be assigned to tough jobs because of a perception that they were weak. The few who did seek counselling through their employer were those working for an organisation whose editorial management insisted that they do so, and where the editorial executives themselves underwent the counselling as an example. In other media organisations, the offers of help were made impersonally, often by email. The journalists interpreted this as conveying a sub-text that the counselling wasn't really important, that they shouldn't really need it, and that it was being offered because the Human Resources department had said it should be.

This interpretation was probably unfounded. There was considerable evidence that, in fact, the offers were made in good faith and that their impersonal nature was part of a deliberate strategy to show that the employer did not wish to know whether staff members had availed themselves of it or not. It was meant to convey the message that the employer was respecting the employees' privacy. But such is the problem with culture: actions are seen in the context of history and habit; misinterpretations flourish, and change is held back.

Some debriefing sessions were held, but they differed widely in content, atmosphere, and effectiveness. Even when they were conducted in a constructive atmosphere, participants preferred to confine their discussions to logistics and equipment failures, rather than to matters of the mind or the heart. Some were conducted in a slightly hard-bitten atmosphere, where there was a sense that this was something that had to be endured, regardless of individual need. None of the respondents said they gave much away in these sessions.

Yet covering the Black Saturday bushfires and their aftermath exacted a severe emotional toll on many media people. When interviewed between three and six months after the fires, few respondents got through the discussions without showing emotion. Whatever their jobs and experiences — seasoned veterans or relative novices; men or women; people from newspapers, radio stations, television channels, or websites; reporters, photographers, or camera operators; those who had been to the fireground or those who had not — all were deeply affected.[1]

Their ability to cope, however, differed widely, and here experience did count. Those with substantial prior exposure to trauma, especially wars and disasters, were able to recognise within themselves the symptoms of their own familiar reactions. They were also able to assimilate the emotional impact more quickly and to remain fixed on the job at hand.

The picture to emerge was of an industry that, while it had come a long way in recognising the trauma caused by covering disasters and wars, still had a lot to learn about how to help traumatised staff.

The causes of their trauma were more subtle than might be supposed when considering some of the hideous deaths that occurred in those fires. Not many of the respondents saw exposed bodies. A few did, and a few more saw bodies in bags or under covers, but most did not. Many were told of horrendous ways in which people had died, and of indescribably awful discoveries made by the emergency-services personnel. So their exposure to physical horror was, to a considerable extent, vicarious. While this was bad enough, and played a part in traumatising them, it became clear from what respondents said that it was by no means the whole story, nor perhaps even the most important part of it. Judging from what they said and from their spontaneous emotional responses during the interviews, the important factors were the shocking scale and intensity of destruction they had observed, the cruel capriciousness of the fires, and their unrelenting exposure to human suffering.

Their immersion in this consuming tragedy was made worse for many by the shock of coming back. It was all so close to Melbourne. Within a few minutes' drive from the fireground, they were transported from a Dantean world of lamentation to what seemed the obscenely serene normality of suburban Melbourne: fast-food joints, traffic lights, and everyone going about their lives as though they were indifferent to what had happened just over the ridge.

This engendered a sense of embittered disconnection between them and the rest of their world, and was something for which few were prepared. It was as if no one understood or could grasp what had happened. Many likened it to returning from a war, where the only people who understood were those who had been in the war, too. This created tensions in the office and, for some, at home. It also altered people's perspective on what was important.

Another commonly reported symptom was a flatness and lack of interest in routine work. Many respondents spoke disparagingly of the usual diet of media stories, as if none of it mattered any more. This mood tended to last for two or three weeks; sometimes, longer. Those who sought professional advice about it were told it was a normal reaction.

The organisation that has done most to change this culture and to provide practical self-care advice to the profession is the Dart Center for Journalism and Trauma. Founded in the United States and with its main office at Columbia University, the centre is led by a journalist, Bruce Shapiro, who was himself the victim of a knifing on the streets of New York. The centre has an Asia-Pacific chapter, led by a psychologist, Ms Cait McMahon, with an office in Melbourne. It conducts seminars and workshops on request across the region, helping those engaged in journalism to understand the nature of trauma and to recognise the signs of traumatic stress in themselves, and introduces them to strategies for self-help.

The center has produced educational DVDs and booklets to help people working in a variety of settings and confronting a variety of stressors. One message keeps coming through in all their materials: Talk about it. Don't bottle it up. However, this big message makes more sense when it is given in a fuller context, allied with personal accounts by journalists who talk about their experiences. They talk about seeing the charred bodies of aircraft-crash victims; of covering the massacre of school children in Beslan, Georgia; of doing a death knock after a motor accident and inadvertently stumbling in on the wake; or of seeing a baby drown in front of its mother in Adelaide's River Torrens. Trauma can occur anywhere, at any time, in the most unexpected settings.

CHAPTER SIXTEEN
A CODE OF ETHICS FOR THE DIGITAL AGE

As we have seen throughout this book, journalism entails an implicit contract with society. By engaging in journalism, a person enters into that contract. The contract says that journalism will provide reliable and relevant information that empowers people to participate in political, economic, and social life. In return, society recognises that practitioners of journalism need certain privileges so they can fulfil that role.

Even though the institutional arrangements for conferring these privileges are still being worked out in the midst of the digital revolution, practitioners recognise that they have obligations both to society as a whole and to the subjects on whom they report. Those obligations derive from certain values that have their roots in the philosophical foundations on which democratic societies are built and which are expressed through journalism's codes of ethics.

An essential value in any democratic society is that of free speech. It is journalism that animates this value and gives it practical effect. From this flows an obligation to speak up in its defence, while at the same time recognising that there are times when it yields to other values. There is also an obligation not to abuse it.

A particular privilege of journalism is the privilege of the platform. It is also the means by which the central power of journalism is exercised. This is the power to portray people and events, to create for the community perceptions of a wider world beyond an individual's own experience.

In democratic societies, the exercise of privilege, power, and the potential to do harm are grounds for requiring accountability to the public. Practitioners of journalism accept this, and are prepared to be accountable for their professional conduct. Practitioners also accept that they have a duty to the public interest.

As we have seen, the public interest concerns matters that affect the citizens' capacity to participate in civic life; public health, safety, or financial security; or the conduct of affairs in which the public have invested trust.

This is not the same as satisfying public curiosity. Where the public interest is invoked as a justification for doing anticipated harm, the public interest needs to be proportional to that harm.

Journalism is distinguished by certain professional norms. One such norm is that information presented as news will exhibit the characteristics of impartiality, and will be free from conflicts of interest. Where such a conflict or potential conflict exists, it will be avoided or declared. Commentary will be separated from material presented as news.

There are other norms: truth-telling, promise-keeping, fair dealing, respect for people, and concern for the vulnerable. They arise in many different ways, and I have discussed them throughout this book. My objective has been to assist in the development of recognised professional standards that remove the ethics of journalism from a kind of relativist jungle towards a consensus about what is the right thing to do.

The values that underpin the ethics of journalism are widely accepted across the Western world, but many practitioners experience difficulty in translating those values into operational decision-making. The approach I have taken in this book is to identify various relevant values, draw from them the principles that are governed by those values, and then express the principles in concrete operational terms.

The code set out below follows this pattern. I intend it to provide a framework for ethical decision-making that people practising journalism can apply, regardless of platform. The digital age presents some entirely new ethical challenges for journalism, as well as some old challenges in new guises. However, the values and the principles they govern are enduring. Departure from these is justifiable only in the public interest.

VALUE	PRINCIPLES
Honesty	When we are acting as a journalist, we declare this at the outset. We tell our subjects truthfully what the story is about, as best we know it at the time. If the story later changes to the person's detriment, we give them a chance to respond.
Truth-telling	We verify information prior to publication. We apply a standard of proof proportional to the seriousness of any allegations we report. We report facts accurately and in a way that gives a truthful impression of their context. We do not exaggerate or 'beat up' the information we have. We do not suppress information that people need for a truthful account. We give an account that is complete as far as we know it at the time. If something later happens that materially alters or adds to what we know, we publish that, too. We correct and acknowledge errors.

VALUE	PRINCIPLES
Fairness	We portray our subjects in a way that is faithful to the evidence we have about them.
	We avoid inaccurate, malicious, cruel, or bad-faith portrayals.
	We avoid distortion or misrepresentation.
	We do not suppress relevant available facts.
	We offer people an opportunity to reply.
	We separate our comment from our news reporting.
Respect	We obtain prior consent from our subjects unless the circumstances make it unnecessary.
	We do not make unnecessary references to people's race, colour, ethnicity, religion, disability, gender, sexual orientation, marital status, or other personal attributes.
	We do not intrude on people's privacy.
	We do not intrude on people's grief.
	We do not exploit people's vulnerability.
	We do not exploit people's ignorance of media practice.
	We do not exploit the content of online social networking sites without the consent of the person who put it there.
Independence	Our decisions about what to publish are based on the journalistic merits of the material.
	Our decisions about what to publish are free of commercial or self-interested considerations.
	Our decisions about what to publish as news have the qualities of impartiality.
	Where propaganda content is inextricable from news content, we minimise the propaganda effect in a way that is consistent with a sufficiently full news account.

VALUE	PRINCIPLES
Confidence-keeping	We make sure that we, and anyone from whom we obtain information, are agreed about the status of the information as on the record, on background, or off the record.
	Information that is off the record is information received in confidence.
	Information received in confidence may not be published or attributed to its source.
	The identity of the source of confidential information is itself confidential.
	Undertakings of confidentiality, including identity of the source, are binding in all circumstances.
Transparency	We do not deceive people about what we are doing.
	We avoid conflicts of interest, and where a conflict is unavoidable, we declare it.
	We tell our audience as much about how we got the story as is necessary for them to make an informed evaluation of it.
	We tell our audience if we have paid for information.
	Correction without acknowledgement of error is insufficient.
Responsibility	We are accountable publicly for our journalism.
	We accept the consequences when we make mistakes or errors of judgment.
	In our decision-making, we take into account the risks and benefits to others.
	Any risk of harm to others is proportional to the public interest to be served.
	We do not place our own interests ahead of other people's.

Free speech	We recognise that all people in a democracy have a fundamental right to freedom of speech.
	We also recognise that free speech gives way in some circumstances to other interests, and therefore is not absolute.
	We recognise that journalism is the main means by which free speech is given practical effect in a modern democracy.
	We recognise that the way we do our work as journalists can promote or hinder speech.
Care for self and colleagues	We recognise we owe a duty to ourselves and our families to take care of our personal well-being, and that we owe a duty of care to those whom we supervise professionally.

MEDIA CODES OF ETHICS AND PRACTICE

The MEAA Code of Ethics

The Media, Entertainment and Arts Alliance is the union and professional organisation that covers people employed in the media, entertainment, sports, and arts industries in Australia. It was formed in 1992, via the amalgamation of a number of industry-specific unions, including the Australian Journalists Association.

This is the alliance's Journalists' Code of Ethics:

Respect for truth and the public's right to information are fundamental principles of journalism. Journalists describe society to itself. They convey information, ideas and opinions, a privileged role. They search, disclose, record, question, entertain, suggest and remember. They inform citizens and animate democracy. They give a practical form to freedom of expression. Many journalists work in private enterprise, but all have these public responsibilities. They scrutinise power, but also exercise it, and should be accountable. Accountability engenders trust. Without trust, journalists do not fulfil their public responsibilities. Alliance members engaged in journalism commit themselves to honesty, fairness, independence, and respect for the rights of others.

Journalists will educate themselves about ethics and apply the following standards:

1. Report and interpret honestly, striving for accuracy, fairness and disclosure of all essential facts. Do not suppress relevant available facts, or give distorting emphasis. Do your utmost to give a fair opportunity for reply.

2. Do not place unnecessary emphasis on personal characteristics, including race, ethnicity, nationality, gender, age, sexual orientation, family relationships, religious belief, or physical or intellectual disability.

3. Aim to attribute information to its source. Where a source seeks anonymity, do not agree without first considering the source's motives and any alternative attributable source. Where confidences are accepted, respect them in all circumstances.

4. Do not allow personal interest, or any belief, commitment, payment, gift or benefit, to undermine your accuracy, fairness or independence.

5. Disclose conflicts of interest that affect, or could be seen to affect, the accuracy, fairness or independence of your journalism. Do not improperly use a journalistic position for personal gain.

6. Do not allow advertising or other commercial considerations to undermine accuracy, fairness or independence.

7. Do your utmost to ensure disclosure of any direct or indirect payment made for interviews, pictures, information or stories.

8. Use fair, responsible and honest means to obtain material. Identify yourself and your employer before obtaining any interview for publication or broadcast. Never exploit a person's vulnerability or ignorance of media practice.

9. Present pictures and sound which are true and accurate. Any manipulation likely to mislead should be disclosed.

10. Do not plagiarise.
11. Respect private grief and personal privacy. Journalists have the right to resist compulsion to intrude.
12. Do your utmost to achieve fair correction of errors.

Guidance Clause
Basic values often need interpretation and sometimes come into conflict. Ethical journalism requires conscientious decision-making in context. Only substantial advancement of the public interest or risk of substantial harm to people allows any standard to be overridden.

Australian Press Council General Statement of Principles

The council is the principal body with responsibility for responding to complaints about Australian newspapers, magazines, and associated digital outlets. The council has published the following general statement of principles. Along with the statement of privacy principles, the general statement is applied by the council when providing advice or adjudicating on individual complaints.

General Principle 1: Accurate, fair and balanced reporting

Publications should take reasonable steps to ensure reports are accurate, fair and balanced. They should not deliberately mislead or misinform readers either by omission or commission.

General Principle 2: Correction of inaccuracy

Where it is established that a serious inaccuracy has been published, a publication should promptly correct the error, giving the correction due prominence.

General Principle 3: Publishing responses

Where individuals or groups are a major focus of news reports or commentary, the publication should ensure fairness and balance in the original article. Failing that, it should provide a reasonable and swift opportunity for a balancing response in an appropriate section of the publication.

General Principle 4: Respect for privacy and sensibilities

News and comment should be presented honestly and fairly, and with respect for the privacy and sensibilities of individuals. However, the right to privacy is not to be interpreted as preventing publication of matters of public record or obvious or significant public interest. Rumour and unconfirmed reports should be identified as such.

General Principle 5: Honest and fair investigation; preservation of confidences

Information obtained by dishonest or unfair means, or the publication of which would involve a breach of confidence, should not be published unless there is an over-riding public interest.

General Principle 6: Transparent and fair presentation

Publications are free to advocate their own views and publish the bylined opinions of others, as long as readers can recognise what is fact and what is opinion. Relevant facts should not be misrepresented or suppressed, headlines and captions should fairly reflect the tenor of an article and readers should be advised of any manipulation of images and potential conflicts of interest.

General Principle 7: Discretion and causing offence

Publications have a wide discretion in publishing material, but they should balance the public interest with the sensibilities of their readers, particularly when the material, such as photographs, could reasonably be expected to cause offence.

General Principle 8: Gratuitous emphasis on characteristics

Publications should not place any gratuitous emphasis on the race, religion, nationality, colour, country of origin, gender, sexual orientation, marital status, disability, illness, or age of an individual or group. Where it is relevant and in the public interest, publications may report and express opinions in these areas.

General Principle 9: Publication of Council adjudications

Where the Council issues an adjudication, the publication concerned should publish the adjudication, promptly and with due prominence.

'Public interest'

For the purposes of these principles, 'public interest' is defined as involving a matter capable of affecting the people at large so they might be legitimately interested in, or concerned about, what is going on, or what may happen to them or to others.

'Due prominence'

The Council interprets 'due prominence' as requiring the publication to ensure the retraction, clarification, correction, explanation or apology has the effect, as far as possible, of neutralising any damage arising from the original publication, and that any published adjudication is likely to be seen by those who saw the material on which the complaint was based.

Free TV Australia
Code of Practice

Free TV represents all of Australia's commercial free-to-air television licensees. Section 4 of its Code of Practice deals with news and current-affairs programs as follows:

Objectives

4.1 This Section is intended to ensure that:

> 4.1.1   news and current affairs programs are presented accurately and fairly;
>
> 4.1.2   news and current affairs programs are presented with care, having regard to the likely composition of the viewing audience and, in particular, the presence of children;
>
> 4.1.3   news and current affairs take account of personal privacy and of cultural differences in the community;
>
> 4.1.4   news is presented impartially.

Scope of the Code

4.2 Except where otherwise indicated, this Section applies to news programs, news flashes, news updates and current affairs programs. A 'current affairs program' means a program focusing on social, economic or political issues of current relevance to the community.

News and Current Affairs Programs

4.3 In broadcasting news and current affairs programs, licensees:

4.3.1   must broadcast factual material accurately and represent viewpoints fairly, having regard to the circumstances at the time of preparing and broadcasting the program;

      4.3.1.1 An assessment of whether the factual material is accurate is to be determined in the context of the segment in its entirety.

4.3.2   must not present material in a manner that creates public panic;

4.3.3   should have appropriate regard to the feelings of relatives and viewers when including images of dead or seriously wounded people. Images of that kind which may seriously distress or seriously offend a substantial number of viewers should be displayed only when there is an identifiable public interest reason for doing so;

4.3.4   must provide the warnings required by Clauses 2.14 and 2.20 of this Code when there is an identifiable public interest reason for selecting and broadcasting visual and/or aural material which may seriously distress or seriously offend a substantial number of viewers;

4.3.5   must not use material relating to a person's personal or private affairs, or which invades an individual's privacy, other than where there is an identifiable public interest reason for the material to be broadcast;

      4.3.5.1 subject to the requirements of clause 4.3.5.2, a licensee will not be in breach of this clause 4.3.5 if the consent of the person (or in the case of a child, the child's parent or guardian) is obtained prior to broadcast of the material;

4.3.5.2 for the purpose of this Clause 4.3.5, licensees must exercise special care before using material relating to a child's personal or private affairs in the broadcast of a report of a sensitive matter concerning the child. The consent of a parent or guardian should be obtained before naming or visually identifying a child in a report on a criminal matter involving a child or a member of a child's immediate family, or a report which discloses sensitive information concerning the health or welfare of a child, unless there are exceptional circumstances or an identifiable public interest reason not to do so;

4.3.5.3 **'child'** means a person under 16 years.

4.3.6 must exercise sensitivity in broadcasting images of or interviews with bereaved relatives and survivors or witnesses of traumatic incidents;

4.3.7 should avoid unfairly identifying a single person or business when commenting on the behaviour of a group of persons or businesses;

4.3.7.1 when commenting on the behaviour of a group of persons or businesses, it is not unfair to correctly identify an individual person or business as part of that group if:

4.3.7.1.1 the licensee can be reasonably satisfied that the individual person or business engages in that behaviour; or

4.3.7.1.2 the licensee discloses that the individual person or business does not engage in that behaviour.

4.3.8 must take all reasonable steps to ensure that murder or accident victims are not identified directly or, where practicable, indirectly before their immediate families are notified by the authorities;

4.3.9 should broadcast reports of suicide or attempted suicide only where there is an identifiable public interest reason to do so, and should exclude any detailed description of the method used. The report must be straightforward and must not include graphic details or images, or glamourise suicide in any way;

4.3.10 must not portray any person or group of persons in a negative light by placing gratuitous emphasis on age, colour, gender, national or ethnic origin, physical or mental disability, race, religion or sexual preference. Nevertheless, where it is in the public interest, licensees may report events and broadcast comments in which such matters are raised;

4.3.11 must make reasonable efforts to correct significant errors of fact at the earliest opportunity. A failure to comply with the requirement in clause 4.3.1 to broadcast factual material accurately will not be taken to be a breach of the Code if a correction, which is adequate and appropriate in all the circumstances, is made within 30 days of the licensee receiving a complaint or a complaint being referred to the Australian Communications and Media Authority (whichever is later).

4.4 In broadcasting news programs (including news flashes) licensees:

4.4.1 must present news fairly and impartially;

4.4.2 must clearly distinguish the reporting of factual material from commentary and analysis.

4.5 In broadcasting a promotion for a news or current affairs program, a licensee must present factual material accurately and represent featured viewpoints fairly, having regard to the circumstances at the time of preparing and broadcasting the program promotion, and its brevity. A licensee is not required by this clause to portray all aspects or themes of a program or program segment in a program promotion, or to represent all viewpoints contained in the program or program segment.

Commercial Radio Australia Ltd Codes of Practice and Guidelines

Commercial Radio Australia Ltd is the national industry body representing Australia's commercial radio broadcasters. Its code of practice for news and current-affair programs is as follows:

Purpose

The purpose of this Code is to promote accuracy and fairness in news and current affairs programs.

2.1 News programs (including news flashes) broadcast by a licensee must:
   (a) present news accurately;
   (b) not present news in such a way as to create public panic, or unnecessary distress to reasonable listeners;
   (c) distinguish news from comment; and
   (d) not use material relating to a person's personal or private affairs, or which invades an individual's privacy, unless there is a public interest in broadcasting such information.

2.2 In the preparation and presentation of current affairs programs, a licensee must use reasonable efforts to ensure that:

(a) factual material is reasonably supportable as being accurate; and

(b) substantial errors of fact are corrected at the earliest possible opportunity.

A failure to comply with the requirement in Code 2.2(a) to broadcast factual material that is reasonably supportable as being accurate will not be taken to be a breach of the Code if a correction, which is adequate and appropriate in all the circumstances, is made within 30 business days of the licensee receiving a complaint or a complaint being referred to the Australian Communications and Media Authority (whichever is later).

2.3 In the preparation and presentation of current affairs programs a licensee must ensure that:

(a) the reporting of factual material is clearly distinguishable from commentary and analysis;

(b) reasonable efforts are made or reasonable opportunities are given to present significant viewpoints when dealing with controversial issues of public importance, either within the same program or similar programs, while the issue has immediate relevance to the community;

(c) viewpoints expressed to the licensee for broadcast are not misrepresented and material is not presented in a misleading manner by giving wrong or improper emphasis or by editing out of context; and

(d) the licensee does not use material relating to a person's personal or private affairs, or which invades an individual's privacy, unless there is a public interest in broadcasting such information.

BIBLIOGRAPHY

Achieving the Balance: a resource kit for Australian media professionals for the portraying of suicide and mental illness, Commonwealth of Australia, 1999.

ANDERSON, D. 'Media Freedom and Responsibility', *Australian Journalism Review*, vol. 11, 1989.

AUSTRALIAN BROADCASTING AUTHORITY. Annual Reports, AGPS, Canberra, 2000–01, 2001–02, 2002–03.

AUSTRALIAN BROADCASTING AUTHORITY. *Commercial Radio Inquiry Final Report*, August 2000.

AUSTRALIAN BROADCASTING AUTHORITY. *Investigation Relating to the Sponsorship of Alan Jones' Program Pursuant to an Agreement Between Telstra Corporation and Macquarie Radio Network Pty Ltd*, April 2004.

AUSTRALIAN BROADCASTING CORPORATION. Editorial Policies: Guidance Note: use in news reports of pictures from social networking sites, issued 19 February 2009.

AUSTRALIAN PRESS COUNCIL. Statement of principles, www.presscouncil.org.au/statement-of-principles.

BARR, T. *Newmedia.com.au: the changing face of Australia's media and communications*, Allen and Unwin, Sydney, 2000.

BEHN, R. D. *Rethinking Democratic Accountability*, Brookings Institution Press, Washington, DC, 2001.

BENTHAM, J. *An Introduction to the Principles of Morals and Legislation* [1780], Dover, New York, 2007.

BENTHAM, J. 'On the Liberty of the Press' in *The Works of Jeremy Bentham*, vol. 2, William Tait, Edinburgh, 1837.

BERLIN, I. *Four Essays on Liberty*, Oxford University Press, Oxford, 1969.

BOK, S. *Lying: moral choice in public and private life*, Random House, New York, 1978.

BOK, S. *Secrets: concealment and revelation*, Oxford University Press, Oxford, 1982.

BOTTOM, B. *Connections: crime rackets and networks of influence down-under*, Sun Books, Melbourne, 1985.

BOTTOM, B. *Without Fear or Favour*, Sun Books, Melbourne, 1984.

BOWMAN, D. *The Captive Press*, Penguin, Melbourne, 1988.

BOYCE, G., CURRAN, J., AND WINGATE, P. (EDS) 'The Fourth Estate: the reappraisal of a concept' in *Newspaper History from the 17th Century to the Present Day*, Constable, London, 1978.

BURNS, C. 'Not Much Power And Very Little Glory', The Third Hugo Wolfsohn Memorial Lecture, 13 September 1988.

CALCUTT, D. *Report of the Committee on Privacy and Related Matters*, HMSO, London, 1990.

CALCUTT, D. *Review of Press Self-Regulation*, HMSO, London, 1993.

CANADIAN BROADCASTING COMPANY. *Acts and Policies*, 2012.

CARLYON, L. *Paper Chase: the press under examination*, The Herald and Weekly Times Ltd, Melbourne, 1982.

CHRISTIANS, C. G., FERRE, J. P., AND FACKLER, P. M. *Good News: social ethics and the press*, Oxford University Press, Oxford, 1993.

CHRISTIANS, C., FACKLER, M., McKEE, K. B., KRESHAL, K., AND WOODS, R. *Media Ethics: cases and moral reasoning* (eighth edition), Pearson Education Inc., Boston, 2009.

COHEN, B. *The Press and Foreign Policy*, Princeton University Press, Princeton, 1963.

Convergence Review Final Report, Report to the Minister for Broadband, Communications, and the Digital Economy, Commonwealth of Australia, Canberra, 2012.

CRAWFORD, N. A. *The Ethics of Journalism*, Alfred A. Knopf, New York, 1924.

CURRAN, J. AND SEATON, J. *Power Without Responsibility: the press and broadcasting in Britain*, Fontana, Glasgow, 1981.

DAHL, R. A. *On Democracy*, Yale University Press, New Haven, Connecticut, 1998.

EMERSON, T. I. *The System of Freedom of Expression*, Random House, New York, 1970.

FOWLER, A. *The Most Dangerous Man in the World*, Melbourne University Press, Melbourne, 2011.

FRIEND, C. AND SINGER, J. B. *Online Journalism Ethics: traditions and transitions*, M. E. Sharpe, New York, 2007.

GALTUNG, J. AND RUGE, M. 'The Structure of Foreign News', *Journal of Peace Research*, no. 1, 1965, pp. 64–90, see also in Tunstall, J. (ed.) *Media Sociology*, University of Illinois Press, Urbana, Illinois, 1970.

GENERAL ACCOUNTING OFFICE. *Block Grants: issues in designing accountability provisions*, GAO/AIMD-95-226, September 1995.

GOGGIN, G. 'Democratic Affordances: politics, media, and digital technology after WikiLeaks', *Ethical Space*, vol. 10, no. 2/3, 2013, pp. 6–14.

GOODWIN, J. AND SMITH, R. F. *Groping for Ethics in Journalism* (third edition), Iowa State University Press, Ames, Iowa, 1983.

GRIFFITH, W. B. 'Ethics and the Academic Professionals: some open problems and a new approach' in *Business and Professional Ethics Journal*, no. 1, Spring 1982.

GRISSO, T. AND APPELBAUM, P. *Assessing Competence to Consent to Treatment*, Oxford University Press, Oxford, 1998.

HALLAM, H. *Hallam's History of England*, vol. 3, John Murray, London, 1884.

HENNINGHAM, J. 'Australian Journalists' Professional and Ethical Values', *Journalism and Mass Communication Quarterly*, vol. 73, no. 1, 1996.

HILLS, B. *Breaking News: the golden age of Graham Perkin*, Scribe, Melbourne, 2010.

HIRST, M. AND PATCHING, R. *Journalism Ethics: arguments and cases*, Oxford University Press, Melbourne, 2005.

HOBBES, T. *Leviathan* [1651], MacPherson, C. B. (ed.), Penguin, London, 1985.

HOCKING, W. E. *Freedom of the Press: a framework of principle*. University of Chicago Press, Chicago, 1947.

HORNE, D. 'But That's Not the Issue' in Schultz.

HULTENG, J. L. *The Messenger's Motives: ethical problems of the news media*, Prentice-Hall, New Jersey, 1985.

HURST, J. AND WHITE, S. A. *Ethics and the Australian News Media*, Macmillan, Melbourne, 1994.

HUTCHINS, R. M. *The Commission on the Freedom of the Press: a free and responsible press*, University of Chicago Press, Chicago, 1947.

JENSEN, J. W. 'Toward a Solution to the Problem of the Freedom of the Press', *Journalism Quarterly*, no. 27, Autumn 1950.

JERICHO, G. *The Rise of the Fifth Estate: social media and blogging in Australian politics*, Scribe, Melbourne, 2012.

KANT, I. *Foundations of the Metaphysics of Morals* [1785], translated by Beck, L. W., Bobbs-Merrill, Indianapolis, 1959.

KEANE, J. 'Lunch and Dinner with Julian Assange, in Prison', *The Conversation*, 18 February 2013, http://theconversation.com/lunch-and-dinner-with-julian-assange-in-prison-12234 accessed 27 July 2013.

KEEBLE, R. L. *Ethics for Journalists*, Routledge, London, 2001.

KENNEDY, D. 'Why WikiLeaks Turned to the Press', *The Guardian*, 27 July 2010, http://www.guardian.co.uk/commentisfree/cifamerica/2010/jul/27/why-wikileaks-turned-to-press accessed 2 August 2013.

KIDDER, R. M. *How Good People Make Tough Choices*, Simon and Schuster, New York, 1995.

KIM, S. Y. H. *Evaluation of Capacity to Consent to Treatment and Research*, Oxford University Press, Oxford, 2010.

KLUGE, E.-H.,'Competence, Capacity, and Informed Consent: beyond the cognitive-competence model', *Canadian Journal on Aging*, vol. 24, no. 3, 2005, pp. 295–304.

KOVACH, B. AND ROSENSTIEL,T. *The Elements of Journalism,* Three Rivers Press, New York, 2001.

LEE, S.T. 'Predicting Tolerance of Journalistic Deception', *Journal of Mass Media Ethics*, vol. 20, no. 1, 2005.

LEIGH, D. AND HARDING, L. *WikiLeaks: inside Julian Assange's war on secrecy*, Guardian Books, London, 2011.

LLOYD, C. *Profession: Journalist*, Hale and Iremonger, Sydney, 1985.

LOCKE, J. 'Two Treatises on Government' [1728] republished in *The Works of John Locke* (twelfth edition), London, 1824.

LULJAK, T. 'The Routine Nature of Journalistic Deception' in Pritchard, D. (ed), *Holding the Media Accountable: citizens, ethics and the law*, Indiana University Press, Bloomington, Indiana, 2000.

MALCOLM, J. *The Journalist And The Murderer,* First Vintage Books, New York, 1990.

MANSON, N. AND O'NEILL, O. *Rethinking Informed Consent in Bio-ethics*, Cambridge University Press, Cambridge, 2007.

MCLUHAN, M. *Understanding Media: the extensions of man*, MIT Press, Cambridge, Massachusetts, 1995.

MCQUAIL, D. *Media Performance: mass communication and the public interest*, Sage, London, 1992.

MCQUAIL, D. *Mass Communication Theory*, Sage, London, 1994.

MARLIN, R. *Propaganda and the Ethics of Persuasion*, Broadview Press, Ontario, 2002.

MAYER, H. *The Press in Australia*, Lansdowne Press, Melbourne, 1964.

MEDIA, ENTERTAINMENT AND ARTS ALLIANCE. 'Code of Ethics: complaints procedures', authorised by Christopher Warren, Alliance Federal Secretary, undated.

MEDIA, ENTERTAINMENT AND ARTS ALLIANCE. *Ethics in Journalism: report of the ethics review committee,* Melbourne University Press, Melbourne, 1997.

MEDIA, ENTERTAINMENT AND ARTS ALLIANCE. 'Journalists' Code of Ethics', www.alliance.org.au/code of ethics.html.

MEYER P. *Ethical Journalism*, Longman, New York, 1987.

MILL, J. 'Liberty of the Press' in *Essays on Government, Jurisprudence, Liberty of the Press, and the Law of Nations* [1825], A. M. Kelly, New York, 1967.

MILL, J. S. *On Liberty* [1859], Gray, J. (ed.), Oxford University Press, Oxford, 1998.

MILLER, H. M. AND HOLDER, P. *Harry M. Miller: confessions of a not-so-secret agent*, Hachette, Sydney, 2009.

MILTON, J. *Areopagitica* [1644], Rivers, I. (ed.), Deighton, Bell, and Company, Cambridge, 1973.

MOORE, M. H. AND GATES, M. J. *Inspectors-General: junkyard dogs or man's best friend?*, Russell Sage Foundation, New York, 1986.

MOSHER, F. C. 'The Changing Responsibilities and Tactics of the Federal Government', *Public Administration Review*, vol. 40, no. 6, 1980.

MULGAN, R. *Holding Power to Account: accountability in modern democracies*, Palgrave Macmillan, Basingstoke, United Kingdom, 2003.

MULLER, D. J. A. *Media Accountability in a Liberal Democracy: an examination of the harlot's prerogative*, unpublished PhD thesis, University of Melbourne, 2005, http://repository.unimelb.edu.au/10187/1552 accessed 1 August 2013.

MULLER, D. J. A. and GAWENDA. M., *Black Saturday: in the media spotlight*, Cussonia Press, Melbourne, 2011.

MULLER, F. *The Making of the Manchester Guardian*, Frederick Muller, London, 1946.

NEWS CORP. 'Code of Conduct', http://www.heraldsun.com.au/help/code-of-conduct accessed 10 August 2013.

NEWS LTD. 'Professional Conduct Policy', http://www.theaustralian.com.au/help/editorial-code-of-conduct accessed 27 March 2014.

NEWTON, L. H., HODGES, L., AND KEITH, S. 'Accountability in the Professions: accountability in journalism', *Journal of Mass Media Ethics*, vol. 19, no. 3–4, 2004.

O'NEILL, O. *A Question of Trust*, The BBC Reith Lectures 2002, Cambridge University Press, Cambridge, 2002.

PARKER, D. *The Courtesans: the press gallery in the Hawke era*, Allen and Unwin, Sydney, 1990.

PATTERSON, P. AND WILKINS, L. *Media Ethics: issues and cases* (sixth edition), McGraw-Hill, Boston, 2008.

PEARL, C. *Wild Men of Sydney*, Angus and Robertson, Sydney, 1977.

PIRKUS, J. AND BLOOD, W. *Suicide and the Media: a critical review*, Department of Health and Aged Care, Canberra, 2001.

PIRKIS, J. AND BLOOD, W., *Suicide and the News and Information Media: a critical review*, Commonwealth of Australia, 2010.

PRITCHARD, D. (ed.) *Holding the Media Accountable: citizens, ethics, and the law*, Indiana University Press, Bloomington, Indiana, 2000.

RAMPTON, S. AND STAUBER, J. *Weapons of Mass Deception*, Hodder Headline, Sydney, 2000.

Report of the Independent Inquiry into the Media and Media Regulation, Report to the Minister for Broadband, Communications, and the Digital Economy, Commonwealth of Australia, 2012.

Reporting Suicide and Mental Illness: a mindframe resource for media professionals, Department of Health and Aging, Commonwealth of Australia, 2011.

RICHARDS, I. *Quagmires and Quandaries: exploring journalism ethics*, UNSW Press, Sydney, 2005.

ROSEN, J. 'Each Nation Its Own Press: nationalism, journalism, and globalism in the age of the web' in Knobel, L. and Rosen, J. *Barons to Bloggers: confronting media power*, The Miegunyah Press, Melbourne, 2005.

ROUSSEAU, J. J. *The Social Contract* [1762], translated by Betts, C., Oxford University Press, Oxford, 1994.

RUSBRIDGER, A. 'Introduction' in Leigh and Harding, *WikiLeaks: inside Julian Assange's war on secrecy*, Guardian Books, London, 2011.

SAMPFORD, C. AND ROBYN, L. 'Australian Media Ethics Regime and Ethical Risk Management', *Journal of Mass Media Ethics*, vol. 19, no. 2, 2004.

SCHAEFFER, P. 'A Compromised Press Delivers Not-So-Hot News', *Theology Today*, vol. 59, no. 3, 2009.

SCHULTZ, J. (ed.) *Not Just Another Business: journalists, citizens, and the media*, Pluto Press, Sydney, 1994.

SCHULTZ, J. *Reviving the Fourth Estate*, Cambridge University Press, Cambridge, 1998.

SEIGENTHALER, J. 'The Privacy Genie's Out of the Bottle', *Media Studies Journal*, vol. 14, no. 3, 2000.

SEYMOUR-URE, C. *The British Press and Broadcasting since 1945*, Blackwell, Oxford, 1996.

SIEBERT, F. *Four Theories of the Press*, University of Illinois Press, Chicago, 1956.

SILVER, N. *The Signal and the Noise*, Penguin, New York, 2012.

SIMONS, M. *Fit to Print: inside the Canberra press gallery*, UNSW Press, Sydney, 1999.

SOUTER, G. *Company of Heralds*, Melbourne University Press, Melbourne, 1981.

SOUTER, G. *Heralds and Angels: the house of Fairfax 1841–1990*, Melbourne University Press, Melbourne, 1991.

STACK, S. 'Media Coverage as a Risk Factor in Suicide', *Journal of Epidemiological Community Health*, vol. 57, no. 4, 2003, pp. 238–240.

TANNER, S., PHILLIPS, G., SMYTH, C. AND TAPSELL, S. *Journalism Ethics at Work*, Pearson Longman, Sydney, 2005.

TEICHMAN, J. *Social Ethics: a student's guide*, Blackwell, Oxford, 1996.

TIDEY, J. *Class Act: a life of Creighton Burns*, Australian Scholarly Publishing, Melbourne, 2012.

TIFFEN, R. 'The Media and Democracy: reclaiming an intellectual agenda' in Shultz.

WARD, S. J. A. *Ethics and the Media: an introduction,* Cambridge University Press, New York, 2011.

WASSERMAN, E. 'Conflict of Interest Enters a New Age' in Wilkins, L. and Christians, C. G. *The Handbook of Mass Media Ethics,* Routledge, New York, 2008.

WIKILEAKS submissions website http://www.wikileaks.org/wiki/WikiLeaks:Submissions accessed 27 July 2013.

WHITE, S. A. *Reporting in Australia,* Macmillan, Melbourne, 1991.

Legal cases

Attorney-General v Guardian Newspapers Ltd (No 2) [1990] 1 AC 109.

Australian Broadcasting Corporation v Lenah Game Meats Pty Ltd [2001] 208 CLR 199.

Board of Trustees of State University of New York v Fox, 492 US 469, 477 (1989).

Douglas v Hello! Ltd [2000] EWCA Civ 353.

Eatock v Bolt [2011] FCA 1103.

Hancock Prospecting Pty Ltd v Hancock [2013] WASC 290.

Jane Doe v Australian Broadcasting Corporation & Others [2007] VCC 281.

John Fairfax & Sons Limited v Cojuango [1988] 165 CLR 346.

Lange v Australian Broadcasting Corporation (1997) 189 CLR 520.

Olmstead v United States, 277 US 438 (1928).

R v Gerard Thomas McManus & Michael Harvey [2007] VCC 619.

NOTES

Preface
1   Kovach and Rosenstiel, pp. 179–198.

Introduction
1   Rosenstiel and Bill Kovach wrote a standard text, *The Elements of Journalism*. This quotation is from an article Rosenstiel wrote in *The Boston Globe*, http://www.boston.com/news/nation/ articles/2004/07/26/whos_a_journalist_take_notes_you_might_be_ surprised/ accessed 7 August 2013.
2   Jericho, p. 104.

1/Lessons from WikiLeaks
1   WikiLeaks submissions website.
2   Keane.
3   Fowler.
4   Goggin.
5   Kennedy.
6   Rusbridger.
7   Kovach and Rosenstiel, p. 17.
8   Ulken, E. *Dialogues: online journalism ethics*, http://jethicsdialogues. blogspot.com/ accessed 7 August 2013.

2/The concept of accountability
1   See, for example, Schultz, 1998.
2   Moore, p. 1.
3   Mulgan, pp. 1–2.
4   *Report of the Independent Inquiry into the Media and Media Regulation*, pp. 104–110.

5   Behn, pp. 123–128.
6   Mulgan, pp. 22–30.
7   Muller.
8   *Report of the Independent Inquiry into the Media and Media Regulation* and *Convergence Review Final Report.*
9   Jericho.

3/Values, principles, and ethical theories

1   Hobbes, pp. 185–222.
2   Locke.
3   Rousseau.
4   Behn, p. 125.
5   Kant.
6   Bentham, *An Introduction to the Principles and Morals of Legislation.*
7   Mill, J. S., *On Liberty.*

4/Four key concepts

1   Locke.
2   Milton.
3   Mill, J.S., *On Liberty.*
4   Mill, J.S., *On Liberty,* pp. 20–21.
5   See, for example, *Board of Trustees of State University of New York v Fox.*
6   *Lange v the Australian Broadcasting Corporation.*
7   Mill, J.S., *On Liberty,* pp. 13–17.
8   See, for example, Ward, pp. 197–205.
9   *Eatock v Bolt.*
10 Hurst and White, pp. 15–18.

5/Impartiality

1   Hocking.
2   Ward, pp. 118–143.
3   Australian Broadcasting Corporation. *Quality Assurance Project 3: Impartiality (News Content),* http://about.abc.net.au/wp-content/uploads/2012/06/QAProject3ImpartialityNewsContentJul2008.pdf accessed 27 March 2014.
4   Australian Broadcasting Corporation. *Sources and Conflicts: review of the adequacy of ABC editorial policies relating to source protection and to the reporting by journalists of events in which they are participants,* July 2008, http://about.abc.net.au/wp-content/uploads/2012/06/SourcesAndConflictsReportJuly2008.pdf acccessed 27 March 2014.
5   See for example, Galtung J. and Ruge M.

6/Conflict of interest
1   Wasserman, pp. 229–241.
2   Tanner, Phillips, Smyth, and Tapsell, p. 187.

7/'The grinder'
1   Ward, pp. 79–86.
2   Kidder, pp. 183–187.

8/Consent
1   Berlin, pp. 135–141.
2   Kluge, pp. 295–304.
3   Kim, p. 4.
4   Grisso and Appelbaum, pp. 31–60.
5   Manson and O'Neill, p. 24.
6   Manson and O'Neill, pp. 84–96.
7   Muller and Gawenda, pp. 140–154.
8   Muller and Gawenda, pp. 141–142.

9/Truth-telling
1   Kovach and Rosenstiel, p. 45.
2   Burns.
3   Bottom, 1985; Bottom, 1984.
4   *Report of the Royal Commission of Inquiry into Alleged Telephone Interceptions*, vol. 1, Commonwealth of Australia, 1986.
5   Silver.

10/Sources and confidences
1   *R v Gerard Thomas McManus & Michael Harvey.*
2   *Hancock Prospecting Pty Ltd v Hancock.*
3   *John Fairfax & Sons Limited v Cojuango.*
4   Hills, p. 459.
5   Hurst and White, pp. 195–215.
6   Miller and Holder, p. 257.

11/Deception and betrayal
1   Luljak, pp. 11–26.
2   Bok, 1978, *Lying: moral choice in public and private life*, p. 13.
3   Malcolm.
4   Gawenda, M. 'The Art of Betrayal', *Media Report*, ABC Radio National, http://www.abc.net.au/radionational/programs/mediareport/23-may-2013/4705896 accessed 31 July 2013

12/Privacy

1   Mill, J.S., *On Liberty*, p. 104.
2   *Olmstead v United States*.
3   Bok, *Secrets: concealments and revelation*, pp. 11–13.
4   See for example *Attorney-General v Guardian Newspapers Ltd (No 2)*.
5   *Australian Broadcasting Corporation v Lenah Game Meats Pty Ltd*.
6   *Jane Doe v Australian Broadcasting Corporation & Others*.

13/Trauma, disasters, and suicide

1   Muller and Gawenda.
2   Pirkis and Blood, 2001; Pirkis and Blood, 2010.
3   Stack, pp. 238–240.
4   *Reporting Suicide and Mental Illness*.
5   *Achieving the Balance: a resource kit for Australian media professionals for the reporting and portrayal of suicide and mental illness*, Commonwealth of Australia, 1999.

14/Online ethical problems

1   http://www.cbc.radio-canada.ca/en/reporting-to-canadians/acts-and-policies/programming/journalism/production-digital/ accessed 8 August 2013.
2   Australian Broadcasting Corporation, 2009.

15/Taking care of ourselves

1   Muller and Gawenda.

Franklin Pierce University

00210480